"To have been the beneficiary of sittir Russell Joyce shine his light for all to see—is one of the greatest gifts of my life. *His Face like Mine* adds to this story. Joyce's brilliant, vulnerable, and fierce exploration of the power of wounds and scars will leave you breathless. If we are healed by Christ's stripes, then this book gives us a door to the doctor's office. Must read."

A. J. Swoboda, associate professor of Bible and theology at Bushnell University and author of *A Gift of Thorns*

"In *His Face like Mine*, Russell Joyce provides us with a guide through the wonder, the searching, the hunger, the longing in our souls to know the Savior. We are invited to find our story in God's countenance and there begin to forge a path toward healing and restoration. Russell's candid tone and delivery are both gripping and holy."

Noemi Chavez, pastor of Revive Church and cofounder of Brave Global

"Some books engage our minds while others help us grow our skills, but every now and then a book will come along that will transform our souls. Russell Joyce has given us that kind of book in *His Face like Mine*. As you read this book, prepare to have your heart enlarged and healed through the beauty of Christ that Russell exposes us to while holding back no punches on the brokenness we all have to wrestle with in order to walk with Christ."

Kristian Hernandez, lead pastor of Hope Astoria Church and founder of the Kerygma Group

"With uncommon vulnerability, Russell Joyce traces a line from his congenital abnormalities through the soulish wounds we all carry straight into Jesus' welcoming, healing, whole-making gaze. More than a line, it's a trail Russell has blazed. He lays out the markers and invites us to follow. I trust Russell's insightful and biblical faithfulness and honest pastor's heart. I love the captivating rawness of the stories he shares. If you ever longed to receive the wholeness of God in any measure—to feel fully loved by the God who is love—read this book."

Randy Remington, president of The Foursquare Church

"Russell Joyce's work is a fresh and vulnerable look at the good news of Jesus' grace. By mingling personal stories with scriptural reflections, he puts forth an embodied apologetic that aims to disarm us all of our false selves, look a little deeper into the depths of our souls, and find the Savior who was there the whole time ready to set us free by his love."

Alan Hirsch, author and founder of Movement Leaders Collective and Forge Missional Training Network

"To know Russ, to walk alongside his story and read these penned words, only verifies the journey traveled. Russell Joyce opens up his scars through a story to invite you in for a closer look and meaningful reflection, pointing you to the hope of not yet. I hope you read this book with an open heart and soul and receive the invitation to become more human, fully flourishing, and welcomed into the arms of a loving God. May you discover the liminal space between the gaze of Jesus upon you and the woundedness within you. May you embrace the love for a face like yours."

Wendy Nolasco, general supervisor of The Foursquare Church

"For anyone grappling with adversity, be it in the form of visible scars or hidden wounds, this book stands as a testament to the possibility of being made whole in Christ. Russell Joyce's narrative serves as a beacon of hope, challenging readers to perceive their own trials through a lens of divine purpose. *His Face like Mine* is an eloquent reminder that, in the hands of a compassionate God, even the most catastrophic events can be transmuted into opportunities for profound personal and collective growth."

Edwin Colon, pastor of Next Step Community Church in Brooklyn, New York

"'Yes, you are broken. But you are not ugly. Do you hear me? There's a difference. I choose you as you are. I will always choose you.' In a visualization exercise, Russell Joyce spoke those words to his younger physically scarred self. Understanding that Jesus and our loved ones embrace us, scarred as we are, is key to this incredible book. I've seldom come across something that speaks to the secret pain I carry. This book brought healing to my soul as it will to yours."

Ralph Moore, church multiplication catalyzer at Exponential

Finding God's

Love in Our

Wounds

His Face
like Mine

Russell W. Joyce

An imprint of InterVarsity Press
Downers Grove, Illinois

For Nathan,

whose friendship is on almost every page,

even if his name is not.

It was a really good group.

InterVarsity Press
P.O. Box 1400 | Downers Grove, IL 60515-1426
ivpress.com | email@ivpress.com

InterVarsity Press® is the publishing division of InterVarsity Christian Fellowship/USA®. For more information, visit intervarsity.org.

All Scripture quotations, unless otherwise indicated, are taken from The Holy Bible, New International Version®, NIV®. Copyright © 1973, 1978, 1984, 2011 by Biblica, Inc.™ Used by permission of Zondervan. All rights reserved worldwide. www.zondervan.com. The "NIV" and "New International Version" are trademarks registered in the United States Patent and Trademark Office by Biblica, Inc.™

While any stories in this book are true, some names and identifying information may have been changed to protect the privacy of individuals.

The publisher cannot verify the accuracy or functionality of website URLs used in this book beyond the date of publication.

Cover design: David Fassett
Interior design: Daniel van Loon
Images: Getty Images: mosaic of the face of Jesus, face in silhouette

ISBN 978-1-5140-0908-6 (print) | ISBN 978-1-5140-0909-3 (digital)

Printed in the United States of America ♾

Library of Congress Cataloging-in-Publication Data
Names: Joyce, Russell W., 1988- author.
Title: His face like mine : finding God's love in our wounds / Russell W. Joyce.
Description: Downers Grove, IL : IVP, [2024] | Includes bibliographical references.
Identifiers: LCCN 2024005012 (print) | LCCN 2024005013 (ebook) | ISBN
   9781514009086 (print) | ISBN 9781514009093 (digital)
Subjects: LCSH: Sick–Religious life. | Suffering–Religious
   aspects–Christianity. | BISAC: RELIGION / Christian Living / Personal
   Memoirs | RELIGION / Christian Living / Spiritual Growth
Classification: LCC BV4910 .J69 2024 (print) | LCC BV4910 (ebook) | DDC
   248.8/6–dc23/eng/20240227
LC record available at https://lccn.loc.gov/2024005012
LC ebook record available at https://lccn.loc.gov/2024005013

31   30   29   28   27   26   25   24 | 12   11   10   9   8   7   6   5   4   3   2   1

Contents

A Longing for Wholeness

God became like us that we might become like him.

Saint Athanasius

The doctors didn't know something was wrong with me until I came into the world. In 1988, the medical technology wasn't advanced enough to catch it. Dad later told me there's a particular horror, the taste of which you never quite forget, when the joy of having a son is immediately replaced by dread as you see the doctors and nurses flush pale in fear. Not even putting me on Mom's chest, they whisked me out of the room to explore my body and investigate what had happened.

On November 17, 1988, in Lexington, North Carolina, I was born with a rare craniofacial disorder called Goldenhar syndrome. Put bluntly, the left side of my face and parts of my body were badly broken.

Nurses would return every few minutes with a new discovery of something broken within me.

"I'm sorry, Mr. Joyce, his left ear is severely underdeveloped."

"His left jaw doesn't seem to be formed, and his left cheekbone is missing."

"He has two holes in his heart. Scoliosis of the spine. Skin tags."

It went on. By the fourth or fifth appearance, the nurses couldn't even hide their tears as they prepared to impart more bad news. Dad retired to the hospital chapel while Mom slept. He never did tell me exactly what he said in that chapel—only that he and God had it out and that he prayed harder than he'd ever prayed before.

My childhood was full of doctor visits and hospital stays. I've lost count of the number of surgeries I've endured. And though my parents knew God gave them this child with a different face for a reason, they still couldn't help but continue the prayer my dad began the day I was born. It was a wonderfully childlike prayer only parents truly know because it was straight from the soul. The words shifted and stumbled and failed. But the ask was pure and powerful and always the same.

Lord, would you make our son whole?

Can you relate? True, my physical abnormalities placed me in a category to which few belong. But isn't wholeness what we all long for?

And don't we all feel that there's a brokenness in our lives, a woundedness in our souls, that isn't quite *whole?*

You're the divorced man or woman carrying your broken marriage around like a millstone for years, feeling as if you're a failure.

You're the student trying to act like everything is all right, even while your soul is abuzz with anxiety and pressure so great that you're sure eventually you're going to be crushed by it.

You're the wunderkind respected by your peers and adored by your family—with a secret so terrible it feels like it's rotting your soul from the inside out.

You're the single person who can't escape your scarlet letter, which no amount of scrubbing or self-talk will erase.

You're in a dry and distant marriage, with all hope gone and cynicism your only reliable companion.

You're addicted to porn and just can't pull away from a cheap connection that you know only deepens the shame.

I could go on, but you get the idea. We all suffer from this sense that there's something wrong. That we're incomplete. That we can't get it right. That we aren't quite *enough*. For God. For others. For ourselves.

The cause of your wounds, like mine, may be something physical you've carried since you were born. It may have come from a less than ideal home life or family. Maybe a season of abuse. A parent who abandoned you, a husband who rejected you, a wife who betrayed you, a church that lied to you, a teacher or coach who belittled you, a friend who turned on you and, yes, even a God who, at least in your eyes, wasn't there for you in your darkest hour.

Whatever wound was inflicted upon your soul, you find yourself feeling painfully less than whole. What's worse:

these wounds calcify into beliefs and attitudes that form habits and lifestyles that only make the pain worse. The unique pain you carry may lead you to inflict painful wounds onto others, too, even if unintentionally. That rejection may lead you to reject yourself and others. That abuse may lead you to abuse yourself and others. That gruesome word spoken over you has spun a web of lies so thick in your mind and heart you can't even begin to cut through it to see the sun shining on anyone's face, much less your own. It perpetuates itself. It grows deeper, darker, lonelier, and wider, making you feel like there's no way out.

Lord, would you make me whole? That's your prayer. That's mine. Though degrees may vary, that's all of us. But as a pastor and, more importantly, a follower of Jesus, I've learned that Jesus came to the earth for one reason: our wholeness. God is not scared away by our wounded souls. In fact, he's acquainted with them even more intimately than we dare fathom. And the wholeness and freedom we're so desperate for are right in front of us if we have the courage to look.

I learned much of this when I served as a church planter and pastor in Brooklyn, New York, from 2015 to 2021. I was twenty-seven years old at the start of that journey and, in many ways, I was trying to learn to ride a bike while putting it together. (FYI, bikes work better if they're assembled first.)

You might wonder what you have in common with the trials and tribulations of a pastor. Let me tell you a secret: even though not all humans are pastors, all pastors are—believe it or not—human! In that life-changing season, God met me in my soul's human woundedness and healed me. I believe he longs to do this in all of us, no matter where we find ourselves.

As we begin this journey together, understand this: our quests for wholeness aren't so much about circumstances or vocation as they are about *perspectives*—ours and God's. Dad said often he'd put me to bed at night, kiss me, and tell me he loved me. No sooner had he closed my door than his heart would begin to pour out in grief, crying for God to heal me. He'd beg God to switch our places. *Heal him. Give me the burden.* He prayed that he'd go to my bedside the next morning to find I had grown an ear, a jaw, a cheekbone.

That was his prayer for years. Until one day, around my twelfth birthday, God spoke back. Dad's heart was heavy, and he began to pour forth the familiar lament: *Lord, heal my son. Jesus, make my son whole. God, you can do anything. Will you please just make my son whole!*

With that last utterance, something moved inside my father. It was fast. But as soon as he felt the shift, a knowledge filled him, spilling upward and outward. The knowledge was an answer to his prayer. It spoke right back to him in no uncertain terms.

Lord, would you heal my son and make him whole? he prayed.

The response: *But can you not see it? I already have.*

Heal my son, God.

Look closer. It's done.

One

The God Who Kisses Our Wounds

O ne night years back, my fiancée, Anna, and I were making out. She lived with six other women in a house in Portland, Oregon, and we found ourselves alone, which didn't happen often. We decided to take advantage of the privacy. We were in our midtwenties, had been together for a year, were recently engaged, and swooning over each other. It was a happy season. In the middle of this moment, she suddenly pulled back.

"Stop that," she said.

I was confused. I hadn't the faintest idea what she meant. I hoped it wasn't my kissing.

"Do you know you always do that?" she asked. "Every time I try and kiss the left side of your face, you don't let me. You either pull my lips onto yours, or you start telling me you love me and how beautiful I am. You won't just let me kiss you."

I was stunned.

"Do you not think I see you?" she asked. "Like, all of you?"

I exhaled as if punched in the stomach. She continued, "Do you not think I love all of you? Let me kiss you."

I sat dumbstruck, cut open by her words. I genuinely had no idea I was attempting to hide the "bad side" and making her kiss what I deemed to be the "good side." I didn't know how to respond or process what she had just revealed to me about myself. I was exposed without any explanation to offer.

"Sit back," she said, her fingers pressing into my sternum and guiding me into the couch. "Look at me."

I did.

She reached out her right hand and began to pull her fingertips across the left side of my face, back and forth, over my brokenness. Her fingertips traced my sunken left cheek where my cheek bone never grew and my bumpy, angular, reconstructed ear. She followed the red line of a giant scar that goes from the edge of my mouth to my ear. Her fingers touched every spot of imperfection on my face.

It took everything within me not to cry out in rage. I felt so vulnerable I thought I was going to faint. My cynicism wanted to spit at her. But since I had never let someone into that vulnerable space, I was terrified. The cynicism was my defense. I hated all of it. *I don't want your pity*, I wanted to scream at her. *I know what I look like. I know how broken I am. Stop patronizing me. I don't need it and I don't need you!* I was so angry at everything and everyone.

But she didn't stop. She kept touching my wounded face. After tracing the outlines of the checkered ridges, misplaced bones, and red scars, she tilted her head forward and began to kiss me. First, she kissed the top of my broken ear. Then the ridges of my ear. Then my underdeveloped jaw. She kissed me slowly and with intention. Her lips would touch as much flesh as possible, holding the pose for as long as it took for me to realize what she was communicating.

She wanted me to *know* and *feel* that she was kissing my wounded face. And she wanted me to know that she was *choosing* to kiss it. No one was forcing her. She wanted to kiss my wounded face because she loved me. Not the me I thought I was or the me I should be, but the *real me*, the one I thought I had been hiding from her. The deformed, broken, weak, deceptive, humiliated, wounded me. She wanted to kiss *that* me.

She wasn't repulsed by my wounds. She wasn't overlooking them. She saw them for what they were, and she knew that there would be no *me* without them and the stories they told of my life. So she loved them. Because they made the *real me*. And she loved the real me.

As she tenderly kissed every inch of wounded flesh on my face—every mark that carried the tragic baggage of all the rejections I had ever experienced, all the stares I had ever garnered, all the teasing I had ever been subject to, all my self-loathing—the shock and rage in my body began to give way. It melted within me. What replaced that rage was an emotion without a name. The closest thing I can call it is grief. *Deep* grief. Yet it transcended even that. I think it was a death. Something was dying in that moment.

I began to wail. I cried harder than I've ever cried in my life. I had always subconsciously believed that if I were ever to be truly seen for what I was, that if I couldn't distract someone by making them look at the good parts of me, then they would reject me. Because that's what wounded people receive—rejection. But now, for the first time ever, I knew I was truly being seen for what I was and that I was freely chosen as I was. Of course, I had been chosen and loved throughout my life by my parents and brothers. But the narrative I believed was that if my family had been honest, they would not have chosen me, not loved me, not kissed me. In my mind, they were overlooking my wounds because they were compelled to do so.

This is why the moment with Anna was so powerful. Anna was not family, and I knew she saw the real me. She called it out. I couldn't hide. She wasn't bound to me by blood. If she wanted to love me, it was her free choice. She kissed my wounded face over and over, and sorrow and pain emptied from my soul. She spoke no words. She didn't stop. In that space of utter brokenness, I was deemed worthy of her love. And I encountered God like never before.

WOUNDS THAT HEAL OTHER WOUNDS

Lord, would you heal my son and make him whole?

But can you not see it? I already have.

Heal my son, God.

Look closer. It's done.

How can God suggest I am whole when clearly, I am not? How can God say I am healed when others' sidelong glances tell me they see someone still in need of healing? How can we be whole unless wholeness for God and wholeness for the rest of us are two different things?

To be clear, this is not a book about my experience having a broken face. It's about how God met me in my soul's wounds found within the stories of my face. It's about how God longs to meet you inside your soul's wounds too. All our souls bear wounds. Some come from brokenness we're born with or born into, which we have to navigate in a fallen world. Some wounds come from pain inflicted on us through others' sinful or ignorant actions. Some wounds we give ourselves, and we don't even know why. And some wounds come from pain we inflict on others, which ends up hurting us in the process too. If we're honest, we can recognize ourselves in all these scenarios. But no matter how our souls come by their wounds, the common denominator is that they all hurt—*terribly*. For those whose wounds are as painful as mine were, I don't know if we really care about what happened, whose fault it is, or why—at least not at first. We just want to know if there's a way to stop the pain. We want to be healed. We want to be *whole*.

As I began to explore the Bible for a way forward, I noticed something peculiar: many, if not most, of the biblical characters were very wounded people, spiritually and physically. Moses had a stutter and killed an Egyptian. Jacob was deceptive and ended up with a limp. David was the youngest of his brothers and driven by his feckless emotions. Paul had a mysterious "thorn in the flesh," which has led to all sorts of hypotheses on whether this was physical, psychological, or spiritual pain—or maybe all three! Regardless, it had a humbling effect on Paul's ministry, his preaching ability, and the shape of the good news of God in the churches he started.

The Bible is such a rich story because God works with our wounded human nature. But it wasn't just that the characters had wounded personalities and pasts; rather, God used those wounded personalities and pasts *specifically* to fulfill his purposes. It wasn't that God used people despite their wounds; rather, he used their wounds *especially* to work out his plans. The wounds weren't baggage; no, they were the very instrument God used to save his world.

That astonished me. I was taught our woundedness was a result of sin—our being separated from God's presence—which is true. I was also taught that God saves us *in spite* of this. However, when I looked closer, I saw no "despiteness" at all in God's dealings. He isn't avoiding our sinful wounds. Rather, he is charging headlong into the most painful elements of our groaning creation. Wherever our most wounded people, behaviors, decisions, and temperaments are found, there is where God is clearly at work—harnessing, healing, delivering, empowering, *saving*—if we are only willing to look. When I realized this, I saw it everywhere. This simple truth—God saves us not *despite* our woundedness but by *embodying* it—is the message of the Bible.

Most importantly, we read it in Isaiah's memorable passage about the suffering servant, who writes of the Savior: "He was pierced for our transgressions, he was crushed for our iniquities; the punishment that brought us peace was on him, and by his wounds we are healed" (Isaiah 53:5). God didn't save us despite our wounds. He saved us *through his own*. The question then becomes, *How do wounds heal other wounds?* The answer to that question may help me understand God's response to my dad so many years ago and how God is doing healing work in all our lives.

LOOKING INTO A MIRROR

Alice Miller, a psychotherapist and expert in childhood trauma, writes about the crucial first weeks of a child's life and the need for the child to bond with his mother. "In the first weeks and months of life he needs to have the mother at his disposal, must be able to avail himself of her and be mirrored by her . . . the mother gazes at the baby in her arms, and the baby gazes at his mother's face and finds himself therein."[1]

Immediate bonding between a mother and a child is incredibly important. Since chemicals like oxytocin are released through skin and eye contact, much is lost when a child is not able to touch his mother's skin and see her face immediately. Miller points out the process of mirroring—how a child gazes upon his mother and mirrors the affections in her. I love the phrase that the child "finds himself therein." He locates his identity in the face of his mother. Likewise, the mother gazes at her child and mirrors the needs she sees in her baby's face.

But what if this ideal scenario is not the case? What if the mother is not emotionally available for the child? Or the mother, rather than serving as a steady fount of love for the child's self-discovery, instead *needs* the love of the child to escape her own pain? Miller answers this question, speaking of how the child gazes at his mother's face, "provided that the mother is really looking at the unique, small, helpless being and not projecting her own expectations, fears, and plans for the child. In that case, the child would find not himself in his mother's face but rather the mother's projections. *This child would remain without a mirror, and for the rest of his life would be seeking this mirror in vain.*"[2]

This is one of the more helpful explanations I've read for the concept of original sin. Sin comes from the Greek word *hamartanō*, meaning to miss the mark.[3] Aristotle used it to describe an archer's arrow that does not strike the bull's-eye. We reduce the concept of sin to lies, greed, or violence; in short, our own actions. But it's deeper than that. We steal because we're afraid of going without. We're afraid of going without because we are not gazing at God our Provider. We kill because we're afraid of not being loved. We're afraid of not being loved because we're not finding love in our Father's face.

Sin, in all its forms—individual, social, institutional, familial, relational, political—represents the ways we've been searching for and not finding our true Mirror all our lives. If, as Gregory the Great wrote, "we are changed into the one we see"[4]—a theological understanding of the process of mirroring—then none of us has ever known a perfect parent or had the chance to mirror a family or a world that allows us to become most fully alive, which is to say, *sinless*. We have been ripped apart from our Heavenly Mirror, and sin is our inability to discover our true selves in this world.

So if you're the college student abuzz with anxiety, perhaps it's because you've never known the perfect peace found in relationship with your Maker. If you're the married person filled with shame, perhaps it's because you never tasted the grace of the Wonderful Counselor who said your marriage isn't saved by your strength or doomed by your weakness.

Perhaps it wasn't *just* the biological process of procreation, as Augustine imagined, which passed down sin to the next generation. Perhaps it was also that none of us had a chance to mirror the living God and find our face in his. Therefore, we have all become stunted and wounded creatures in a stunted and wounded world.

But what of Jesus?

We read in Colossians that Jesus is the visible image of the invisible God (Colossians 1:15). Could it be that the reason Jesus of Nazareth, the poor carpenter turned itinerant prophet, healer, and preacher, is so compelling to billions is that he was a human being who did not miss the mark of the ideal human condition? That he was a human who gazed at God's face, our true Mirror, and therefore was able to grow into the perfect image of Love himself, without mar or distortion? That in Jesus we see human wholeness— and our woundedness? If wholeness is unimpeded mirroring between God and us, then what we see in Jesus is that woundless, whole relationship. We see a sinless life.

But that is not all we see. Jesus' life culminated not how we imagined a sinless life would but in a gruesome, humiliating crucifixion. By his *wounds* we are healed. I wonder if God is trying to reveal that he sees us as we really are. On the outside we look put together and strong, but on the inside, doesn't it feel, in a way, like we're hanging on a cross, bleeding out from the wounds we've acquired living in a broken world with broken mirrors and broken relationships? It's as if we're split open from how terrible we can be to one another, how held captive we are to the agency of the evil one—suffocating, weakening, and ultimately waiting to die.

If mirroring is how we're transformed, and none of us ever had the chance to mirror God, then could Jesus on the cross be God's attempt at mirroring *us*? Athanasius, a fourth-century pastor, seemed to think so. He wrote that "God was made like us so that we might be made like him."[5] We couldn't find our face in his, so instead, he found his face in ours. God took on wounds, just like us, that our wounds might be healed and made whole, just like him.

THE KISS OF GOD

Which brings me back to Anna kissing my face. When she called me out, asking, *Do you not think I see all of you?* I was stunned because truthfully, no, I did not. It took me a few years to process that moment, but here's what I can now articulate. I believed that Anna was overlooking my brokenness in her attempt to love the "loveable parts" of me—my virtue, my character, my personality, my mean scrambled eggs, that sort of stuff. I believed that only the right side of my face was worthy to be kissed. So when she tried to kiss my left side, my subconscious replied, *No, no, let me help you. That side is unfortunate and it cannot be saved. It's too far gone. The right side is the side that deserves love.*

If we really take in what it means that Jesus would end his historical existence with such a death, it should shock us, like Anna pulling back and saying, "Stop that! Do you not think I see all of you? Do you not think I love all of you?" That is the message of Jesus on the cross. It is God mirroring us, saying, *Stop it, world. Enough is enough. I see all of you. I love all of you. I am with you in your worst, which is to say your true, condition.*

Yet notice, the message isn't enough on its own. If Anna wanted to communicate her love for the real me, she could not say, "Let me kiss you," and then kiss only my "good side." Instead, she demonstrated she loved all of me by kissing the worst parts of me. She channeled her love through what I believed to be the most unlovable part of my very being.

And when she did that, I knew she loved all of me. Because if she can love me through my worst, if she can kiss the ugliest parts of me as a free choice, then I know there is no part of me too ugly for her love.

This is why the story of Jesus astonishes me so much. Jesus came to communicate God's love for the world—a very wounded world that hides many of its wounds, even from itself, much like I thought I was hiding mine from Anna. To get through to us with the message of God's love, one we scarcely believe, Jesus had to communicate that love directly through the world's wounds. Not around them or despite them, but *through* them. He had to mirror the real us.

When you see Jesus on the cross, you see him experience your secret addiction as his own. He feels the neglect you suffered as a child. He hears those ugly words spoken by your parents, siblings, and friends as if they were spoken to him. He knows the way you cruelly treated your family, and he feels their pain and yours. He knows how you've led a self-absorbed life rejecting those closest to you, and he feels that rejection and loathing. He wants to join you in those most shameful places, not watch from afar. He wants to feel them with you, alongside you. He knows the precise pain that these wounds have caused you. And he wants to know it fully because he wants to be with you, the real you, not the you you're pretending to be or the you that you wish you were.

On the cross God brings his love, through Jesus, onto the true human condition of brokenness, sin, suffering, and death. "God made him who had no sin to be sin for us, so that in him we might become the righteousness of God" (2 Corinthians 5:21). In Jesus, we know there is no amount of woundedness too ugly for the love of God. The cross assures us of this because God's love has kissed the wounded human. And as Jesus hands over his life to death, God's powerful love joins us even in our coffins. The power of the cross is the God who kisses wounds so that we may know we are loved, not despite but *with* our wounds, because his love has been channeled *through* them.

On the cross, God kisses our real face.

YOUR REAL FACE HAS SCARS

Yet as beautiful as that is, we're still not done. Infection makes a wound painful and tender. That's why when Anna began to touch the left side of my face with loving intention, I wanted to scream out in rage for the wound of my broken face and all the history associated with it was being touched. But the more she kissed me, *the more her love joined me in that place*, the more the infection was cured and its power emptied. When a wound is healed it does not stay a wound, nor does it go back to pre-wounded flesh. It can only go forward as a new manifestation of what it was.

It becomes a scar.

Our history remains. We were separated from God. We have never mirrored our Maker and so we split each other open on this earth. But because God joined us in our brokenness, sin, and death, our wounds caused by these forces no longer have power over us. The infection is cured and the wound becomes a scar—one that no longer hurts but is still very real. Lest we forget, when Jesus emerged from his tomb victorious, he did not emerge unscathed.

He went to his disciples and showed them his scars.

Look at Jesus. Put your finger in his hands. Touch his side. God will always be the God with scars—because if we are to live, we cannot go back to an unwounded state of existence. We can only go through it, which is why God's power is most clearly revealed in scars. His scars are a sign of his strength, that he defeated the powers separating our souls from his love. This is how Paul can sing, "Where, O death, is your victory? Where, O death, is your sting?" (1 Corinthians 15:55). For he sees on Jesus' body what sin can do to a person—and yet, Jesus stands alive.

In 2 Corinthians 12, Paul recounts how God sent him a thorn in his flesh so he would not become conceited about how much God was showing him spiritually. Paul pleaded with God three times to take it away. We can all relate to this: begging God to take away some burden, some memory, some practice that keeps causing discomfort in our lives and souls. But the Lord said no. Rather, God told Paul, "My grace is sufficient for you, for my power is made perfect in weakness." Paul then said, "Therefore I will boast all the more gladly about my weaknesses, so that Christ's power may rest on me. That is why, for Christ's sake, I delight in weaknesses, in insults, in hardships, in persecutions, in difficulties. For when I am weak, then I am strong" (2 Corinthians 12:9-10).

According to Paul, God's love and power are made real not because he pulls the thorn out of the flesh but because we find him in the middle of the pierced flesh, which can no longer destroy us. We hold up the scars of what were once wounds and say, "They have no more power over me, for God has met me in them and healed me there by his love." Weaknesses, insults, hardships, persecutions—the world doesn't see good in these yet, but those who have found Jesus there will. The person struggling with addiction who does not shy away from her past but no longer is held captive by its pain. The divorcé who humbly shares how the pain of his failed marriage revealed the unfailing love of God. The perfectionist who has been released by Jesus, who met her in her imperfection. These are all scars that must be lifted up to the world as signs of the sufficiency of God's grace and power. If we boast in our scars long enough, we give others permission to come out of their own hiding and receive the kiss of God. We give others a chance to be healed too.

I was too ashamed to let Anna kiss my scarred face, believing it to be unworthy. Little did I know that on the last day it will *only* be my scarred face that is worthy of kisses. For scars are the sign that God's love has entered and made whole again.

MIRRORING THE CRUCIFIED JESUS

Because we don't mirror the living God in our lives, we mirror something else and turn that thing into our god. If we don't know that God has entered our broken marriage, our negative self-talk, our depression and anxiety, then we're still desperately looking for a perfect mirror to escape our inner wounds. That perfect mirror could be a job, a spouse, an idyllic family, a bazillion Instagram followers, political ideologies . . . the list goes on. We continue searching for some idea or thing or person in this life and try to *will ourselves* to be healed by becoming just like it.

There is nothing unique about this desire to make a savior into our own image of what we think will save us. It's as old as time—the human instinct to serve and adore a mirror who accords with what our society values and wants.

Paul addresses precisely the same situation in his letter to the Corinthians. After acknowledging the factions that have developed in the new church community, he expresses that the centerpiece of their very life is Christ. No one else was crucified for them. He goes on to say that God has used the foolish things in this world to shame the wise, so they should not be surprised if people don't understand what they say about the Son of God. Then he writes, "Jews demand signs and Greeks look for wisdom, but we preach Christ crucified: a stumbling block to Jews and foolishness to Gentiles, but to those whom God has called, both Jews and Greeks, Christ the power of God and the wisdom of God" (1 Corinthians 1:22-24).

Paul is saying that the Jews will always want a miracle-worker Savior while the Greeks will always prefer a Socratic Savior, in the same way every nation has always fit Jesus into their ideological preferences too. And it's so tempting to acquiesce to them. It's tempting to talk to a room full of Greeks about the wise, philosophical teachings of the rabbi. It's tempting to talk to Jews living in Asia Minor about the apocalyptic, Torah-saturated signs that Jesus performed. It's tempting to tell those of us living in the Western world that Jesus' power makes us immune to sadness and will lead us toward material blessing, or that his compassion means there's no need for us to undergo the pain of transformation. And to be sure, in some ways, we would not be completely lying. But the point, says Paul, is that *we cannot start there.* If we do, we lose God's real power. "We always preach Christ crucified, a stumbling block to Jews and foolishness to Greeks [not to mention despicable to Americans], but to us, those being saved, it is the power of God ... *so that no one might boast in the presence of God*" (1 Corinthians 1:23-24, 29, author's paraphrase).

Why? Because the reality is that the world—Jews, Greeks, and everyone else—is full of wounded souls bleeding out from its separation from God. Yet no one wants to admit that. Only God knows that's who we really are. He's the only one who loves us enough to save the real us. So if you're looking for God's love, you won't find it in your strength, your success, or some fantasy of a utopian community, but in your brokenness, your failures, *your own wounded face.*

I wish I could tell you from the moment Anna kissed my wounded face I have never doubted her or God's love. But that's not true. I have found within my soul a myriad of wounds that reveal I do not want to find God in my weakness. I want to be strong. I want to be admired. I do not want people to see my fears, my insecurities, and the ways I have hurt Anna and loathed myself.

I want them to see my intelligence, my successes, my happiness, my virtue signaling—in short, *the right side of my face.* Yet if I do this, I empty the cross of its power. I have no good news to offer anyone. And it rises up in my soul too. Often, when I have subconsciously been focusing my attention on the world's form of boasting, I will discover within me fear, anxiety, vileness, depression, and self-absorption. When that happens, Anna notices it as well. She'll force me to sit down on the couch and, just like before, she'll kiss the left side of my face. Every single time I'll feel irritation and anger come to the surface because I know what this action represents, and it is humiliating. She is forcing me to remember the *real me,* the one I am tempted to hide from everyone, even myself.

But then the weight of this truth washes over me—I am loved not despite my wounds *but through them.* She sees the real me and she chooses that me. I have nothing to prove. I have nothing to earn. I have nothing to lose. And I am reminded again that scars are God's beautiful signs to a world that isn't yet truthful about its own wounded face.

In the pages to come, I want to tell you the story of a God who meets us in our wounds, kisses them, and turns them into scars, encouraging us to boast in them. It is a story deeply needed in a time when we find ourselves afraid to boast in our weaknesses, afraid to reveal our wounds to one another, afraid to say the wrong thing, afraid to be real in a culture that is performative, afraid to show grace when our society demands perfection, afraid to show our real faces and how much pain we're carrying. This is the story that played out time and again for me as I tried to find my way as a young pastor filled with doubts about what, exactly, I was doing and who I actually was.

Anna and I moved to Brooklyn and started a church. Ours is not a story of strength, conquest, or glamour but of weakness, brokenness, and grace. Because I believe that you will most clearly see God in my story when you see my soul's wounds on the cross. When you see the grotesqueness in my shame, the perversion of my heart, and the depths of my deception, and yet you see me still praising the mercies of God's grace because he has joined me in those places with his love, then I believe you will encounter God's power too. My prayer is that by doing so you will find the courage to let God come near those wounds in your heart and offer the message he has constantly delivered to me:

Russell, you are truly seen for who you are, and you are freely chosen by me.

My prayer is that the church will become a beacon of hope because all of us will be known for boasting about our greatest wounds, our most embarrassing failures, no longer ashamed. We will be known as people who point to our scars, for in so doing, we point to the scars of God. My prayer is that in our community, we will be a people who, like Anna, invite others to show the left side of their faces and receive the kiss of Christ.

When we do so, my prayer is that we would begin to understand what wholeness has always meant for God. That just like my father, when we are tempted to cry out, *God, would you please heal us and make us whole?* we would see Jesus mirroring us, pointing to his split open body, his poured out blood, and his face like ours, saying, *But can you not see it? I already have.*

Two

The God Reminding Us Who We Are

In February 2015, a month after we married, Anna and I visited New York City. We had no idea where we would be after my graduation from seminary that May and, through a string of connections and circumstances, New York City became an option. We took a trip on the coldest weekend that winter to pray and seek God's direction. It was a Saturday—snowy and still, with little flakes salting Brooklyn's cobblestone streets that overlooked a gray East River. We were meeting a South African couple named David and Liza, friends of friends, who had moved to the city a few years earlier on the prompting of God to serve the church there.

The coffee shop where we met was an old, converted warehouse with expansive windows and poles throughout. Anna and I listened to David and Liza share their story. They had left Cape Town and came to New York with no job, no guarantees of ministry, and only a religious visa, which severely limited their financial situation, along with three young children.

"Why did you come in the first place?" Anna asked.

They shared how something had slowly become unsettled in their spirits back in Cape Town. They couldn't name it, and they knew such a move made no logical sense; their lives were abundant, and the church they served was flourishing. Friendships were deep and their marriage was good.

"But something began to shift in us that said *this isn't it*," Liza said. *"There is something else."*

They remembered the voice that had unsettled their hearts and knew their life's call was to that voice. They opened the door to what God might do, and he rushed in. Over time, they surrendered everything. They moved their entire lives to a new city and country. They lived in a terrible apartment their first year, where people in the units above and below them were engaged in illicit affairs. Their hope waned, but they remained constant. They remained faithful. They recalled the words God spoke about their need for trust in this new place.

As they told their story, Anna and I were consumed with emotion. Not because we felt sorry for them and all they had endured, but because we wanted what they had. They *knew* God and his voice. Their identity was secure. Though they weren't perfect, there was power in their lives shown through their faithfulness, their obedience to the call of God, because they remembered what his voice sounded like.

As the snow fell peacefully that sleepy Saturday in February, Anna and I shared how we were in a similar place of trying to listen to God and take steps toward him even though, like them, this burgeoning tug toward New York City made no sense. They smiled and listened. Then David laughed, leaned forward, and said, "Look. If your hearts will allow you to go anywhere else, you should go there. But if not, then remember the day when the call became certain and final. And ensure you both have it etched into your memories. Because you will have many moments in this journey where you will have to recite back the story of the day God confirmed in your hearts, *this is where you are to be.* Write it down. Remember it. Do not forget that moment."

In the weeks that followed, God spoke through text messages from friends who had no idea what we were considering, through divinely placed sermons and Scriptures, and through confirming conversations with loved ones. We didn't know where we would live or what we would do, but we knew God wanted us to join his work in New York. So nine months later, in September 2015, we moved.

REMEMBER ME

Have you ever noticed that one of the most important commandments God gave his people—whether Israel in the Old Testament or the church in the New Testament—is to remember him (Deuteronomy 5:15, 1 Chronicles 16:12, Ecclesiastes 12:1, John 14:26)? It's the central ingredient baked into the Passover and Lord's Supper—*eat and remember me.* Gather the fam over and over, lay out the spread, and remember the founder of the feast. Do it again. Now, do it again. Now, do it again.

Why such a tedious request? Abraham Heschel described faith as remembering what it was like when we had faith— a cynical yet quasi-biblical statement. To believe is to remember believing in God. To remember again, and again, and again. And somehow, in the remembering, we are set ablaze with faith once more. We are held secure in God's will for us and the world. Why is God so obsessed with his people remembering him, recalling what he's done in the past, and continually doing so? Perhaps it has to do with how quickly you and I forget everything.

Isn't it true? God answers your prayer, and ten days later you're sure it was all a mirage. Or he provides financially in a miraculous way, but when the bills come next month, you're sure it's time to start clipping coupons. Or maybe you had a moment with God as a teenager, but the tides of life have pushed you so far you can't even recall if it was real.

The science surrounding memory is fascinating. The ancient Greeks thought of memory as impressions on wax tablets. You and I often think of our memories like RAM on a computer, ready to be downloaded at whim.[1] The similarity in these examples is that our memories are secure, ready to be accessed and replayed. This view is called the standard theory of memory consolidation, which has held court for the last hundred years. Except recent discoveries show this isn't how memory works at all.

In a series of experiments conducted at New York University, a team conditioned rats to fear a loud noise by following it up with an electrical shock. After many days, the rats were terrified whenever the sound came, the fearful memory etched into their brains just as the standard theory proposes. So the experimenters moved into phase two. Knowing memories are formed by electrical signals between neurons, the researchers wondered what would happen if they stopped the neurons from doing their job. As reported, "When [scientists] blocked the rats from *remembering* their fearful memory, the *original* memory trace also disappeared. After a single interruption of the rats' remembering what happens when hearing a loud sound, their fear [of loud sounds] was erased."[2]

This seems to fly in the face of everything we've ever believed about our memories' permanence. But the conclusion has been backed up by subsequent studies. Memories are not kept in your brain the same way you keep your documents in a file cabinet—safe, secure, untampered with, always the same. They do not exist as independent realities. Rather, *your memories are only as real as the process of remembering them.*

This is the secret. With each passing recollection, your brain is recalling the memory all over again *but as if it were the first time.* Details get modified; other details forgotten; new details created. You'll never get back the original memory.

It's like when you save a Word document on your computer. Document one becomes document two becomes document forty-four. And when you open the forty-fifth version of the document, reading the story again for your friends around the campfire, document forty-five is not a revision of document one. Rather, forty-five is an edit of forty-four. There is no document one, and there hasn't been for some time. The theory is now called memory *reconsolidation* because our memories are always impressionable to new information, or new interceptions, that fundamentally change the memory, our emotions toward it, and our *identities* forever.

We're all like rats, our souls conditioned from childhood to fear the noises of this world, knowing a shock is following. If only there were an *interception* that could remove our paranoia and transform our identities into something else.

Good news: there is.

AN IDENTITY CRISIS AT THE HEART OF OUR STORY

The book of Exodus has been called a metanarrative—a story revealing a universal pattern.[3] Exodus has a lot to teach us about who God made us to be and why we find it so difficult to live into that identity. So I think it highly significant the story kicks off with, "Then a new king, to whom Joseph meant nothing, came to power in Egypt" (Exodus 1:8).

Why does God want us to remember him? Because our universal story opens with someone who forgot his people. And when Pharaoh forgot Joseph and Joseph's God, he enslaved and murdered Joseph's children. There are grave consequences when people don't remember who God is. These consequences don't have to be as extreme as slavery and death, either.

Consider Moses, who is born a Hebrew but raised an Egyptian. This creates an identity crisis for him. His blood says he is one nature, yet he is raised in an environment that disregards his Hebrew identity, has forgotten his God, and tries to tell him a different story about himself.

Are we not the same—born into a world that seems at odds with what is within us? We are destined to suffer and die, yet riding in the car with the top down on a summer day, we're sure that suffering and death are not what we were made for. Everything around us says this world is all there is, and yet our souls are not satisfied with that answer. Voices suggest our existence is meaningless, yet we all desperately seek meaning for our lives. *Why does Egypt not satisfy Moses if it's all he's ever known?* Because before he was an Egyptian, he was a Hebrew. Why does this world not satisfy us if it's all we've ever known? *Because we were not created by the world; we were created by God.*

"All of the interesting characters I've ever worked with—including myself—have had at their center a feeling of otherness, of homesickness," writes Anne Lamott.[4] At our collective core is a hunch that something isn't right in this world. We're not home here, which is confusing because the world is the only home we have ever known. In our quiet moments of complete, vulnerable candor, we realize our souls long for the perfect Mirror, and it's not here.

At our depths is the nagging sense that we have forgotten some-thing key to our identity and the desperate longing to remember what it is. We come face to face with Moses' identity crisis. We are Hebrew children raised in an Egyptian empire. We are children of God raised in a world that has forgotten God.

As C. S. Lewis writes, "Our life-long nostalgia, our longing to be reunited with something in the universe from which we feel cut off, to be on the inside of some door which we have always seen from the outside, is no mere neurotic fancy, but the truest index of our real situation."[5] We are wounded, looking for wholeness. We are homesick, searching for home. But we never find it. We go from relationships to jobs to drugs to traveling to comfort to mindfulness to marriage to kids to all sorts of things, trying to fill the void at the center of our souls. But we still feel incomplete. The peace doesn't last. The itch comes back. We look for a different mirror. We seek out another voice. *But at our depths is always the nagging sense that we have forgotten something key to our identity and the desperate longing to remember what it is.*

THE DEEPER ECHOES OF GOD'S VOICE

In 2015, Anna and I had gotten connected with a beau-tiful network of churches called Hope Church NYC, and I was the pastoral resident at the Astoria, Queens, location. We had begun a home group in our apartment, made some wonderful friends, and started a cinematography business. It was great. But that December, the church network asked Anna and me to plant the next Hope Church in Brooklyn, which meant big changes.

Brooklyn, though adjacent to Queens, might as well have been on the moon. My friend Jason said, "We'll basically never see each other again." Anna and I knew God's voice had brought us to New York to join in his work, but we couldn't help wondering: What if this wasn't "of God"?

We told our network we would spend the Christmas season praying about it. That Christmas we stayed with Anna's family in Portland, Oregon. One evening, we visited the church where we fell in love when I was an intern. It was a young community that met in an old Episcopalian building—classic Portland. Anna and I loved this church. It featured dark stained-glass windows and wooden light fixtures shining down on a dingy carpet and rickety pews.

I'd first noticed her in this room. She was saying a prayer during service, and I remember thinking she looked really hot in her hoop earrings. (I was *quite* holy at the time!) Out the doors and straight across the vestibule was the fellowship hall, where we would set the tables with white cloth and retro purple-and-gold napkins for dinner. The church shared a meal every Sunday before service. Like Communion, that was also part of the liturgy. We ate together before we worshiped together. The room was terribly hot in the summers when I interned there.

During our first conversation at one of those tables, we talked about hiking, and I asked if she would take me sometime since I didn't have a car. The next summer when we were engaged, she would help me with my intern duties washing dishes and setting the tables before service. Because we had a fondness for this church, being back a few years later was surreal as we now took Communion on a cold December evening with the prospect of starting our own church across the country in another city brewing in our hearts. There were a lot of memories bubbling up.

As we walked forward in line to receive the bread and wine, I began to rub Anna's shoulders. We were both sensing a holiness in this moment, remembering this tradition in this place. How many times had we taken the elements, gotten up from the pews, and moved forward to once again remember that Jesus was in charge of our lives? If he was strong and selfless enough to sacrifice his body and blood because he loved us, then he was strong enough to be in charge.

But this time it was different. Though we were in Portland, we had Brooklyn on our minds and Hope Brooklyn in our hearts. We both felt a heaviness. Dipping the bread into the cup, we knelt at the altar and prayed. Our arms intertwined, our hands holding purple-stained bread, our heads hunched, and overcome with emotion, we began to cry.

It was an emotion that embodied sadness, hope, anticipation, and an abiding sense of God's presence all in one.

It was joy. The poet Rilke thought of joy as a visitation.[6] Author Christian Wiman spoke once about a friend who sought out pleasure but never joy because joy destabilized her. Joy demands a response because it is never contingent on the circumstances. Pleasure is logical. But joy comes when you aren't looking for it. It sneaks up on you, and you can never trace it back and explain why it happened. *Joy is a visitation, an interception.* Joy is when the veil is pulled back even though we have done nothing to pull it back, when the deeper echoes of God's voice emerge amid a world conditioned to fear because it has forgotten him.

We were fearful. This call to plant Hope Brooklyn was happening a lot sooner than we had imagined. We had only been in the city four months. Neither of us had done anything remotely close to starting a church—much less in New York City. Anna missed Portland and her family. We loved our church here. This all felt so massive. And yet as we cried out for courage and perseverance, for God to pave the way and to slam doors if this was not his will, deep joy was the only response.

You are my beloved, he seemed to say through the joy of his presence. *I'm so proud of who you are.* We stayed at that altar for a couple of minutes, telling God all the things he already knew—our inadequacies, the lack of strategy in this situation, our new fragile marriage. We were being visited by something that defied our circumstances. We were tasting unmerited delight and a light on a path that seemed too much for who we were. Yet, we knew we were being called out. So right there at that altar, we said yes and didn't look back.

God had to call Moses out too: "One day, after Moses had grown up, he went out to where his own people were and watched them at their hard labor" (Exodus 2:11). To remind us of who we are, God has to get us quiet enough so we can hear him. *God calls us out*—out of the palace, out of Egypt, out of our comfort zone, just *out*. Things go wrong. Things break down. Things zig when you thought they would zag. Perhaps it's the Lord trying to call *you* out. Why? Because he wants to remind you of something.

When Moses was called out, he saw something that struck a chord within him: a Hebrew being beaten and forced to work harder by an Egyptian. Without realizing it, Moses saw an element of God's nature, and his brain and heart recognized that forced labor and abuse weren't right. He got a glimpse of what he had forgotten, and he heard a deeper echo of a neglected voice. He remembered to whom he belonged, even if he didn't have the language for it yet.

James K. A. Smith calls these moments *transcendence*.[7] They are experiences in which we feel awoken to something, as if we are remembering what we had forgotten. The veil lifts and for a moment, we see clearly. These moments puncture our clouds of confusion and hint at another reality in this world that says we desire meaning for our lives because there *is* meaning to our lives; we don't feel at home in the world because this world *isn't* our home. It's a sunset hike in a season of doubt, watching the golden orb transform the skies into colors beyond description and knowing all this beauty couldn't have been an accident. It's a dinner with friends in a season of loneliness that is so sweet and whole that time stops and you look up to see hours have gone past, sure that you were made for an eternal moment like this. It's gazing into the eyes of your new son or daughter, flooded with a joy so breathless it's as if the entire world has existed for this one moment.

These are moments of awe, joy, beauty, or the recognition of justice bucking against the injustice of our societies. These are moments of transcendence when something deeper than our very breath, something more real than our consciousness, fills the gaps around and within us, and a voice seeps into our souls, escaping upward and outward.

Or perhaps these moments of transcendence emerge in a warehouse coffee shop on a snowy February day when complete strangers share their story, listen to yours, and speak in such a way that your heart feels entirely possessed by a presence so holy and deep it seems like you are in eternity. Or maybe it's when Joy visits you at an altar you know so well with a meal you take every Sunday, awakening you to some new significance that is even deeper than the moment or the fear. *At our depths is the nagging sense that we have forgotten something key to our identity and the desperate longing to remember what it is.* Transcendence is when, for a moment, we hear and remember the voice that we have forgotten. It is when that voice speaks sweetly to our fear-conditioned souls and, at least for that moment, we remember we were made to be whole.

THE TRUE INTERCEPTION OF OUR SOULS

Three months later, in late February 2016, we were preparing for Hope Brooklyn's first vision dinner—a gathering of people interested in hearing the vision for this new church. The joy that was so comforting in December had entirely disappeared. My fear, anxiety, and neurotic obsession that became part of my identity from living in a world that has forgotten God came back. I had no idea how to start a church and was suddenly very insecure about the whole ordeal.

My friend Drew, who's like the godfather of starting churches, recommended I distribute an evite to get a pulse on attendance and start casting vision. So I sent out an evite to as many people as we knew who lived in Brooklyn and were affiliated with our network. This was the first chance I got to witness how insecure my identity truly was, to see how tightly the world's voice gripped my heart. As our first vision dinner approached, I could not stop checking the evite RSVP list every five minutes. With every green *yes* check mark, my heart leaped. And with every *no*, my stomach dropped. Very quickly I became enslaved to the list, addicted to knowing who was coming, who was not coming, who was telling who on Facebook, and if the person they told would even show up.

You know how it feels if you're a parent desperate for enough likes on Instagram to validate that you're doing a great job raising your kids, or if you need excitement and adrenaline to mask how hurt you are by a father you could never please. You know how it feels if you need your significant other's constant affirmation to assuage your fear that maybe you're not worthy of love. We all do this. Our souls long to remember precisely who we are. But since we can't, we search for other voices to affirm us and give us a secure identity. And these other voices—whether well-intentioned or not—are never enough.

When I had coffee with people, I would make internal notes on questions they asked and how many times they nodded. I was obsessed with trying to read people. When Anna and I had meals with others to talk about the new church, the first question I would ask her when they left was, *Do you think they're in or out?* She would shake her head and kindly say, *Babe, you can't try and read people like that.* Of course, she was right. But I couldn't stop myself. There was something inside me that could not stay away from this type of thinking.

Here is the truth: I judged all these insignificant, nonexistent cues not because I wanted to love and serve the people I was meeting and present Jesus to the neighborhood, but because I was insecure. I realized in those early days that starting a church was a proposition not just on what people believed of God but also what they thought of me. Later,

I realized it came down to this: if Hope Brooklyn lived or died, *I believed it was a verdict on my legitimacy as a person and whether I was worthy of love.* That sounds wild, doesn't it? Yet that belief was deep inside me.

What I couldn't tell Anna, because I didn't yet fully know it, was that it wasn't about the church. It was about *me*. Do they accept *me*? Am *I* worthy? If I am, they'll come. If I'm not, they won't. In many ways my work in life was my desperate, sinful attempt to convince people I was worthy of their love. And I craved *their* love because I had forgotten *God's* love.

Let's go back to the rats. In the experiment, the discovery was so incredible because a single injection in the rats completely erased the forty-five days of conditioning they underwent to make them fear the sound associated with an electric shock. One interception of the fearful memory, and the fear was gone! Our memories, even our tragic ones, are only as real as our last recollection of them. Every time we remember moments in our life, we are reading and revising the last saved version of that document according to new information in our world and about us.

The basic and shocking premise is that our memories, even the deepest and worst ones, can be augmented with new information. Like the rats, with an appropriate interception in the moment of remembering something, our lives, our worldviews, and our very *identities* can be changed. Nothing is final. Nothing is beyond redemption. Our brains, and our memories, are constantly being reshaped.

The memory of the teacher who said you'd never amount to anything, which has spawned countless hours of self-doubt, is not permanent. The secret shame you have carried and are certain spells condemnation for you can be interpreted another way if someone breaks in to say it can. All those words spoken to you about your worth, your lovableness, your purpose, and your future are not fixed nor final. Though our identities are weak, and our emotions shot, we can be brought back. We just need an interception.

Not transcendence, which only hints at the voice we've forgotten, but a true encounter. We need to hear God's voice speak to us while we remember the moment our identities were shattered. When our partner told us, "I've never found you attractive," we need God to say, "I find you beautiful." When our parents didn't show up to our most important games or recitals, we need to instead see Jesus sitting in the front row. That's the only way our identities have a chance at redemption. But here's the question begged by such realities: *Is God willing to do that?*

Moses tended sheep in Midian for forty years, and God said nothing. That season of silence was crucial—even though God had not yet given Moses a new identity, Moses was no longer letting Egypt tell him who he was, either. Note the perfect irony of God. He first made Moses a shepherd of sheep before calling him to shepherd God's people. Israel needed a shepherd because even when they were called out of Egypt, the voice of Egypt was still vying for their hearts, dissuading them from believing God loved them and would take care of them.

Watching sheep, Moses learned not just how to save them from wild animals but how to coax them into greener pastures when they didn't want to go. He learned how to discipline the obstinate ones. He learned to spend whole days doing nothing but sitting and being with his sheep. He learned the lifestyle of his new identity, even though God hadn't spoken it over him yet. He learned love.

Seasons of silence are our crucibles, forming in us habits and rhythms that will be needed when the time comes for God to show up and remind us who we actually are.

And right on time, God appeared. God showed up in a burning bush to send Moses as his representative to deliver his people out of bondage and into freedom. He was sending Moses, the deliverer, to remind the Israelites who they were—the free and loved children of Yahweh.

But Moses didn't believe God, which means every day of those forty years was necessary for Moses to even have a chance at accepting his identity. Moses recounted to God all the reasons why he should not be the deliverer, all the wounds in his identity forged through his memories of Egypt's voice. He said he was unworthy. He said the people would be unwilling to listen and go. He said God would be too unknown, too unremembered, to be trusted. He said his voice and speech were too uncouth. Moses listed to God all the stories the world had ever told him about himself and how unworthy he was to do anything remotely close to delivering an entire nation of people.

This is our story. God shows up and says, "You are my beloved who I am so delighted with," and we say, "You've got the wrong guy. Look at my shame. Look at the left side of my face. See my wounds. See what I have done. See who the world says I am. I could not possibly be loved by you like you say I am." It's not that God hasn't spoken; we just keep responding that we don't believe him. So God has to go even deeper into our wounded identities.

During our initial months of hosting vision dinners at Hope Brooklyn, I was also still the pastoral resident at Hope Astoria—and growing increasingly agitated, depressed, anxious, and afraid. During my time there, a group of people from the local halfway house began attending because of a guy at the house named Patrick, who was a Christian. Stocky and bearded, he was a happy man with a habit of relapsing, being placed in a new rehab facility, and bringing the people there to church, where they would inevitably encounter Jesus and start following him. It was remarkable. I began to wonder if relapsing was part of Patrick's evangelistic approach.

What was more astonishing about this season was that we had done nothing at Astoria to reach these people. No outreach, no volunteering, no text messages, no evites, no Twitter come-ons. No mental, emotional, physical, or financial effort expended on our part. Literally, out of nowhere, this guy started bringing a crowd of people to the church—and six of them became Christians and wanted to get baptized.

To be candid, this made me a little angry at God because at that time I was expending tremendous amounts of emotional, physical, and financial energy trying to reach and engage people in Brooklyn. Yet we did nothing in Astoria, and people were being baptized right and left. My priorities, of course, were misplaced; I wasn't as worried about glory for God and bread for the hungry as I was about self-affirmation. And this scenario worked against my needy identity.

I remember the baptism class that I led with the group. Most had never been to church. I had written a really nice lesson connecting baptism to Moses leading Israel through the Red Sea and to Paul's understanding of the nature of sin in Romans. It was poetic. I was pleased. To which when I finished my piece, one guy named Martin raised his hand and sheepishly asked, "Who's Moses?"

Having no idea where to go from there, I looked at the group and asked, "Why do you want to be baptized?" Martin told me about his nine-year-old daughter, who he had disappointed by not showing up to her birthday parties and canceling when it was his weekends to have her because he was high. He shared how unworthy he felt because of how much he had failed her. But one day at church as we were singing about Jesus, he just felt so ... *loved.* He couldn't explain it; he had never encountered that before. As he thought of Jesus he felt overwhelmed by acceptance, as if he had done some heroic thing and was being recognized for it. At the same time, he thought of his daughter and the ways he had failed her. But the acceptance didn't go away. The joy and love didn't fade but even increased in intensity.

"Whatever this is," he said, "I want more of it. If it's possible that Jesus sees how terrible I am and still loves me—man, that's crazy!"

Another guy named Luis, soft-spoken and monotone, shared how he was raised by his grandmother. She loved him and would pray for him, but he was terrible to her. He was full of anger at the world and so, because he couldn't find the culprit of his pain, he took it out on himself. He nearly drank himself to death. The halfway house was part of his parole.

He started coming to church because of Patrick (who sat in the back of the class grinning the entire time) and his devoutly Catholic grandmother, with whom he'd lost contact. One day as the church was singing about Jesus, he looked around, just like Martin, and for the first time he wasn't angry but felt as if he liked these people. What's more, he felt as if God liked *him*. The sermon was about how Jesus took on all the anger of a world that hated God—yet God never hated the world. It shocked Luis because he knew that was his story. After the service, he called his grandmother for the first time in a long time.

For the next two hours of the baptism class, story after story, people named what was happening in their hearts. They described how they had felt so discarded, how they had given up on themselves and believed they were nothing more than addicts. But here in this church they felt cherished, like God was happy they were here and didn't want them to leave, even though he wasn't denying their addictions or avoiding their mistakes. They felt loved and accepted not *despite* their mistakes but *with* them.

God was *intercepting* their deepest memories of pain. He was capturing their wounded identities and changing their stories forever. He was intervening in what the world told them they were—addicted, ruined, disparaged, unlovable—and speaking new information into those memories, kissing their wounded faces, and healing them. Because now here was God, ruined, disparaged, and unlovable, just like them.

Even as they felt all these things, Joy appeared in the memories of their worst days, wrapping them up like a warm blanket. Jesus was kissing their wounded views of themselves, joining them in those horrible memories not to condemn but to redefine, to say, *even here I still love you with all my life*. They heard God's voice reminding them of who they were: the beloved of God. They knew it was true even as they struggled to believe it, even as they held up to Jesus all the reasons why they shouldn't be loved, just as Moses did.

But God pushed their doubts aside, saying, "You are my child." From here on out, they would have to reconcile the world's condemning voice with the deep hope that their lives were more than the sum of their mistakes. They were worthy to live and to love, because Jesus loved them at their worst and did not condemn them but joined them there with compassion and grace.

All that information will trace the neural pathways of their brains again and again as they remember who they are. And on that day, in that baptism class, Jesus intercepted all our plans and revealed something even better: in all our shame and amnesia, we are—every last one of us— still his beloved.

The day of the baptism came and Kris, the pastor at Astoria, allowed me to do the honors with the group since I had built relationships with them. The band sang a beautiful song of Jesus overcoming the powers of sin and death. The group sat in the first row, clothed in swim trunks and T-shirts, nervously waiting their turn. One by one, I invited them up while the guitars strummed softly and the rest of the congregation sat watching and praying. Those being baptized stepped into the metal tub, warm water sloshing over the sides and soaking my jeans and shirt. I clasped their hands and leaned over the tank.

They began to breathe heavily, sensing the gravity of the moment—the interception of their lives. I prayed with each person, asking God for protection, thanking him for his love and their eternal nature as his beloved child, and commissioning them to keep Jesus before them and know nothing could remove them from the Father's hand. They were no longer separated from God. He had entered their wounded life just as they were because he'd also had a wounded life and recovered from it. God had joined them in their addiction and defeated it to love them there. They were kissed in that wounded place and healed. Did they renounce Satan and all his lies to make them forget who they were? They did. Did they confess Jesus Christ as the Deliverer, the one whose life, death, and resurrection from the dead signified the victory of God's love in their wounded souls? They did.

Then I baptize you, my brother, my sister, in the name of the Father, the Son, and the Holy Spirit. I tilted them backward into the water as they clutched their noses. The community cheered when they emerged, freshly baptized and dripping. Every time one of them surfaced, I, too, felt my heart being washed and heard the voice of the Spirit reminding me, *This is church.* I was so overcome I had to hold back tears. This was the first time I had been seized by God's love since that December in Portland. My identity had been drowning in anxiety, struggling with the dawning realization that I was thinking about it all wrong: in starting Hope Brooklyn, I had focused on myself being validated by others instead of others being validated by Jesus.

Until then, I hadn't known of this insecurity within me, though it had slowly been revealed over the last few months. These wounds—which I hadn't seen and which required God to call me out to show just how frail my identity was—were now being used by God. Even after I saw how little I trusted God's love, look! *God was still using me.* He worked in these beautiful lives, and I got to play a role in leading them to baptism. I was handed such a high honor in being able to share this moment with these people as God entered their identities with his boundless love.

A new and unconquerable edit had occurred in the story of their lives. The resourcefulness of God was that as he intercepted them for the first time, he also intercepted me for the fiftieth or hundredth. I now finally noticed what was happening. I realized he had met me through David and Liza to get us to move to the city. He had plucked us at the altar that Christmas in Portland. And he was intercepting me, again, right then.

Remember!

A TASTY SCAR FOR OUR NEW IDENTITY

At our depths is the nagging sense that we have forgotten something key to our identity and the desperate longing to remember what it is. The journey of our lives is God's attempt to silence the voice of the world and tell us who we really are in his eyes. It is a journey to make us whole again. To make us his again. He captures our identity with love that never runs dry, with a sacrifice only he can make. He sets us free from enslaving powers that do not have our abundant life in mind. With our every realization of how broken we are, of how much of the world is still in us—whether through addictions or betrayal or self-absorbed insecurity—God reminds us that his love and power are deeper still. He reminds us that he sees and chooses us, that he still calls us his sons and daughters. But because our memories are only as real as they are remembered, we forget these interceptions. We need a constant reminder of them. We need a daily notice that we are truly seen and freely chosen. We need a scar to boast in so that no matter how ugly the world says we are, we can remember the voice of God that tells us a different story. In the same way an interception at the precise moment can edit our worst memories, we need a constant interception in our *best* ones, too, to keep this new identity at the forefront of our hearts and minds.

In Exodus 12, before Israel is completely delivered out of Egypt, before they cross the Red Sea, before God even strikes down the firstborns, he gives them a command. He tells them that on this night, the night he's going to intervene and save them, they are to celebrate with a meal. He gives them the full recipe—a sacrificed lamb, blood over the doorframe, bread without yeast, bitter herbs—and tells them how many days they are to celebrate and that it is to be an annual feast so that each generation's children will know who God is and be swept up in the interception of who they are too. This is so they keep the memory of their identities as God's people on the tip of their tongues.

I love the idea of celebrating God's radical salvation with a feast. Professor Rachel Herz points out that our senses of smell and taste are uniquely sentimental because these are the only senses connected directly to the center of our brain's long-term memory.[8] That's why the smell of bonfires takes us right back to summer camp and the taste of cornbread sends us straight to Thanksgiving, as if our entire being is present in those days again just with one whiff or bite.

In the earliest Christian tradition, after a new group of people was baptized, the very first thing they did was share the Lord's Supper.[9] Up until this point, people who did not confess Jesus were allowed in the worship service, though they could not receive the Lord's Supper. But when they were ready to be baptized, they would prepare for a year with spiritual training and be baptized naked. Then they would be clothed in a white robe, be anointed with oil, and sit down with everyone else for a delicious feast. As Paul tells us in 1 Corinthians 11, the Lord's Supper originally wasn't a cardboard wafer and over-sweet juice. It was a *supper* of bread, meat, and wine. This theme is all throughout Scripture. After the prodigal son returns to his father, he is given a robe, a ring, and a feast (Luke 15). The image of heaven is constantly likened to a wedding reception (Revelation 19).

I don't think God is hiding his hand at all. Salvation is delicious! Healing, though costly, is ultimately the most nourishing thing that can happen to your soul, and it's well worth the price to God. It's as if God is saying, "I know how your souls and memories work. I know what forces are still vying for your attention. So here on out, whenever you remember how I intercepted your identity and got to the root of your wounds with my love, I want you to eternally associate it with the most wonderful parts of being alive. I want you to constantly smell the aroma of my grace, perpetually taste the sweetness of my acceptance, and diligently chew on the cost of my sacrifice. Let this memory, this broken, scarred memory of who you are in my eyes, fill your mouth and your belly with the goodness of *me*. And then hold the broken bread and poured out wine up high, and give thanks for these scars—yours and mine."

We have forgotten we are the beloved of God. He has reminded us and intercepted our wounded souls with his own wounds, giving us a new memory and restoring within us our true identity. He has chosen to fasten this memory within us with a feast. Every time we eat this bread and drink this cup, we are reminded all over again whose we are and what it cost to bring us back home. The scarred God meets us in his scarred meal.

So, boast in the scars of Jesus. Boast in your own. Boast and remember him because through them, he will intercept others' lives and the world will remember his voice. Let such an aroma of grace come through your scars that others wonder how something seemingly so painful can smell so much like fresh bread.

Three

The God Who Limps In as a Guest

In 2015, Edwin Colon and I grabbed breakfast at a Dominican restaurant called Yayo's. He led a sixteen-year-old church plant on Third and Schermerhorn named Next Steps Community Church, which ministered greatly to recovering addicts. A Puerto Rican from Greenpoint, Brooklyn, Edwin has salt-and-pepper hair and the most empathetic face you'll ever see. When someone else is happy, his face beams. When they're sad, his brow disappears into his skull. Everyone at Yayo's knew him.

At this breakfast, which happened before Hope Brooklyn and even before we were part of the Hope Church NYC network, Anna and I were still praying about where God wanted us to land and in which community we would serve, and we were discussing the possibility of working with Edwin. So that morning we shared a breakfast of eggs, plantains, and fried cheese with him as he animatedly forced us to order the café con leche because, according to him, it's the best thing you'll ever drink. I told him then and I'll tell you now—it's just coffee with milk; no offense to Yayo's or Dominicans anywhere.

Edwin shared his story. He had come from a broken home, started smoking weed at eleven, experimented with alcohol and harder drugs soon after, and was a full-blown addict before he graduated from high school. In a radical conversion, he became a Christian in college. Overwhelmed that the grace of God would love him with his addictions and long to deliver him all the same, he wanted to serve this God. So he started a Bible study with his buddy, also a recovering addict, in his living room.

His ministry model was simple. His family invited people into their house to have a meal and a place to sleep. They'd lock their bedroom doors as a precaution, but in the morning they would lead Bible studies and sing songs with whoever was still there. In time, the Bible study outgrew the apartment and became a church. Sixteen years later, they were ministering all over New York City with multiple con-gregations and had a thriving church of incredible people.

As Edwin spoke, my heart came alive. It was an amazing story of God's grace meeting people in their wounds and loving them, working out a plan that was gnarled and broken but also beautiful. He and I were both passionate people, and it was clear we shared a deep love for Jesus' church. But throughout the breakfast, I was confused.

"Edwin, your church sounds amazing," I said. "But it's obvious that this is a reality far from my own. I have no experience with recovery ministries. Why are you interested in Anna and me working with you and your church?"

He sat back and crossed his legs. Letting out a soft snort, he gestured behind him at the floor-to-ceiling windows where we gazed out onto Fifth Avenue.

"Look around you, man. Thirty-floor apartment buildings have gone in all around us. Thousands of new residents who can afford them will be moving in. That Barclays Center is a symbol of what will continue to take place. I mean, a Shake Shack just went in across the street. A Shake Shack! You know you're not in Kansas anymore when a Shake Shack goes in."

He lowered his hands, and his face turned somber. "The neighborhood is changing, man. I need a white guy in skinny jeans."

OPPORTUNISTIC EYES AND A DECEPTIVE NAME

In his book *The Christian Imagination*, Dr. Willie Jennings traces a compelling and depressing story of a version of Christianity that was intertwined with the colonization of the Americas. The Europeans in the fifteenth century struggled to see the New World as communities but rather as underdeveloped resources waiting to be maximized.[1] They saw these places as untapped potential. They saw purpose. They saw power. They saw fields ripe for the harvest and the taking.

Colonization is a huge topic. If you're in the mood for an academic book that will make you think and pray, I recommend this one. But for our purposes, I wonder if the idea of exploiting others for personal gain yet justifying it as somehow looking out for them, too, is an impulse we can all relate to. We've betrayed friends to gain popularity saying it will raise their status in the long run. We've neglected spouses and kids in the pursuit of our careers thinking their economic interests are what's most important for them. We've lied to avoid trouble or embarrassment or to preserve our position in a group rationalizing that it's just easier for everyone that no one ever knows. Any time we see a situation as a means to get what we want, even if it means hurting another, we are embodying the logic Jennings describes. Instead of using the power God has given us to create life, we steal, kill, and destroy. And though the accolades pile up, there's a hidden cost to our souls. We know these costs in the stillness of the night when we're left with nothing but our fears.

Genesis 32 demonstrates these dynamics. Jacob is the second son of Isaac, the son of Abraham, and will be known as the father of the twelve sons who become the twelve tribes of Israel. In fact, because of this story in Genesis 32, Jacob's name will be changed to "Israel." But that hasn't happened yet. Right now, Jacob is still Jacob, and he's heading home after a long time away among the people of his mother's family.

It wasn't the greatest sendoff a decade-and-a-half ago. As the second son, Jacob was not the heir of his father's inheritance. Rather, that role was to be occupied by Jacob's older brother, Esau—until Jacob stole Esau's birthright. One day when Esau came home after hunting, incredibly hungry, Jacob offered him a bowl of soup if Esau would give him his birthright. On paper, not the best of trades. However, Esau was "famished unto death" in that moment and agreed. Jacob saw a demand and rose to meet it at the market's current valuation of the commodity.

I like to think of Jacob as those guys in the New York City subway selling bottles of water on the worst summer days. It's already a hundred degrees outside, and with no air conditioning underground, packed in with other people waiting for the train, you're practically sweating your clothes off. Those guys station themselves on the platform with a twenty-four pack of bottled water in a cooler full of ice. Are those waters worth two dollars a bottle? Most certainly not. Am I going to buy one? *Every. Single. Time.* Those guys get it. Like Jacob, they are opportunists. Hustlers. Businessmen. Whatever you want to call them.

Another time, Jacob strapped furs to his arms and deceived his blind father by pretending he was Esau to extract his father's blessing, which was a really big deal in those days because the blessing was reserved for the eldest son. As you can see, Esau and Jacob have a complicated history—holidays are weird.

Esau naturally grew very angry at his brother. Fearing Esau might kill Jacob, their mother sent Jacob to her side of the family to get a wife. Jacob then married two sisters, Leah and Rachel, and acquired a great deal of wealth, flocks, herds, and servants, oftentimes through deceptive means.

By the time we reach Genesis 32, Jacob is leaving his in-laws and, with his wives, children, flocks, herds, and wealth, heading back to his homeland. He's nervous because his brother Esau has become a powerful figure in the land, and rumors are spreading that Esau had been tipped off to Jacob's return and is coming out to meet him with a band of people. Their last interaction not being a pleasant one, Jacob is assuming the worst. He splits his wives, his flocks, and his servants apart to preserve some futurity in case it all goes horribly wrong. Now alone, having crossed the ford of the Jabbok, Jacob decides to spend the night.

One interesting detail about Jacob—his name means "the supplanter." Other ways of defining it are "the overreacher" or "the one who takes what isn't his through deceptive means." He sees opportunity and deviously uses his power to grab it even at the expense of others.

Now, bookmark Jacob and return with me to New York and Edwin. Though he and I would ultimately discern that Next Steps Community Church was not the best fit for Anna and me, he was close with the Hope Church NYC network, and so we became friends. Fifteen months after that first meeting with Edwin, in the spring of 2016, Hope Brooklyn was starting to form. We had hosted Hope Brooklyn's vision dinners at a friend's house in the Fort Greene neighborhood and were continuing those monthly until the summertime. Anna and I were still living in Queens while I was a pastoral resident at Hope Astoria, but I tried to spend a lot of time in Brooklyn walking the neighborhoods, meeting people, and praying for guidance and vision for where the church would ultimately be.

Meanwhile, Edwin and I continued to build our relationship. He hosted a monthly prayer meeting for Brooklyn pastors on Fridays that I attended. He and I would drink coffee and chat afterward. Interestingly, he said, as the neighborhood changed, more new churches started popping up. And generally, though not exclusively, they were led by church planters who were not from the city. People like me—white guys in skinny jeans.

The tough part was that sometimes it seemed like these outside pastors didn't acknowledge the work Edwin and Next Steps were doing or the work other churches had been doing in Brooklyn for a long time. Edwin needed their partnership, but it didn't feel like they needed his. Instead, they were so focused on their own thing as if to insinuate that God hadn't been at work in Brooklyn until they came along. That may not have been the case. But that's what it felt like, and it was hurtful.

It was as if they were using the power God had given them, but in such a way that they were looking out for themselves without regard for those who had been in the city laboring for a while. For example, some of the newer churches planned a worship night and invited a number of other similar churches in the city. But there were also a lot of churches overlooked, most of them like Next Steps— smaller communities that were a bit grittier, less affluent, and comprised of longtime Brooklyn residents. It seemed as if the newer churches were capitalizing on a moment to reach people, but in the process they were overlooking others, leaving them to fend for themselves.

I assured Edwin I wanted Hope Brooklyn and Next Steps to work together in this city as partners, and I hoped my presence at the prayer meetings assured him of that. But even as I listened to him, I still felt the weight of my own lack of awareness. I totally would have gone to that worship night if Hope Brooklyn existed and if I had been invited, without a second thought. I also felt the fear and pressure to get something done, even if I had to do it on my own power and it hurt some people in the process. I didn't want to make the same mistakes and yet, I knew I already had and would continue to.

Here was the wound within the power God had given me. I would use my power, and had used my power—socially, economically, racially—to get what I wanted even if it took away from another person or group of people. I'm sure to some degree, Edwin had too. We all do it because we're all products of a mindset that encourages us to use our power to get our own way, even if doing so intentionally or un-intentionally exploits someone else or another group. It's not that we hate them (most of the time); it's that our impulse is to look out for ourselves.

And many times, we don't see the consequences of these decisions. We don't recognize how our choices to better ourselves are connected to the painful exploitation of others. You want to be there for your friends, but when the popular crowd invites you to the party, you go without considering how your friends might feel discarded. Maybe when you serve on a group project at work you're praised as the main contributor, and you decide it isn't that big of a deal, not realizing that others believe better of you, and worse of the rest of the team, than deserved. Or conversely, maybe you sign a petition or give money or vote a certain way, thinking you are on the side of justice only to later feel the pain of knowing you were deceived.

God is working in each of our lives, and though we want to join him, we still have patterns of behavior inside us that haven't changed. Like Jacob, we lie to our parents or elders to steal a blessing, we deceive friends, family, and neighbors to get ahead, and we look out for ourselves first even if others are destroyed. These moments are wounds in our lives. When we come face to face with those we have hurt, whether we are aware we have hurt them or not, we may be frozen with shame and indecision, not knowing how to handle the situation.

You would love for these stories to go away. You'd love to atone for them or find closure, and certainly not make them worse. You'd love to move forward, not denying the past but no longer being bound by it. I wanted to walk forward planting Hope Brooklyn with faith and love, not shame and fear. But I didn't know what to do with the past nor how to honor new friends like Edwin without hurting him or others more in the process.

How do we use the power God has given us to add to his garden instead of ripping up flowers to create our own warm, controlled flowerbeds?

LOVE THAT FEELS LIKE A WRESTLING MATCH

Jacob was aware of his wound too. He was aware that he'd lived up to his name—"the deceiver." That's why he was so scared upon hearing the reports that Esau was coming out to meet him. Jacob knew what he deserved, and so he split up his family and remained alone by the Jabbok to spend the night. It's then we're told, "and a man wrestled with him till daybreak" (Genesis 32:24).

Out of nowhere there is a mysterious figure wrestling with Jacob all night. People have speculated this man is Jesus, but in this story we don't know. He is some representative of God, and evidently, God's representatives aren't afraid to wrestle humans all night long. Neither combatant, however, gains the upper hand. Amazingly, the supplanter cannot supplant his new foe. He cannot steal or deceive or overpower as he is used to doing to get his way. But neither is he being destroyed. They are in a stalemate.

The story continues:

> When the man saw that he could not overpower him,
> he touched the socket of Jacob's hip so that his hip was
> wrenched as he wrestled with the man. Then the man
> said, "Let me go, for it is daybreak."
>
> But Jacob replied, "I will not let you go unless you
> bless me." (Genesis 32:25-26)

Let's pause to recap the scene. Jacob is a deceptive man
with a wounded past. He has stolen much and profited from
it. He's afraid to meet his brother since he imagines he will
justly receive retribution for what he's done. Heading home
alone, he wrestles with a representative of God. They fight
for hours and the divine figure cannot, or will not, overcome
Jacob. As the sun begins to rise, the divine figure touches
Jacob's hip and dislocates it. Yet even still, Jacob refuses to
let the man go until he receives a blessing from him. When
animal furs and deception won't work, good old-fashioned
determination is in order. It's an odd scene, to be sure. But
there is something incredible happening, especially in the
Hebrew language in which the story was written—three
things in particular.

First, there's the word translated "wrestle." It is the
Hebrew *avaq*, which in its noun form means *dust*. To wrestle
is "to join in the dust."[2]

Second, there's the divine figure dislocating Jacob's hip.
The word "hip" is the same one used to describe the loins

or upper thigh of the patriarchs. The upper thigh, the "palm of the hip," is around the area of procreation. So it has the figurative sense of a person's *power to create life.*[3]

Finally, there's verse 25, which reads, "and Jacob's hip was put out of joint" (ESV). The verb for "to put out of joint" can be interpreted as "to tear away" or "to alienate." It's used eight times in the Old Testament, and half of those times it is translated not as "dislocate," as it is here, but "impale."[4]

Putting it all together, a messenger of God gets dusty with Jacob. As daybreak approaches, the messenger impales Jacob's loins (not a fun image). He strips away the power that Jacob once deceptively used to secure life on his own terms. Jacob, realizing he has been bested, holds on until he receives a blessing, an assurance of safety since he realizes he now has no power to assure his own. This, I contend, is God's kiss of Jacob's wounded, and wounding, power. It is a painful love—impaled loins usually are—but love all the same that empties his past of its infected, and infective, nature. It sets him on a new trajectory with a new way to use his power, trusting God and for the good of others.

JESUS' WAY OF USING POWER

We've all lied and manipulated our way through to get ahead or to get what we want. Like Jacob, we've betrayed others to protect ourselves. We've closed our eyes to suffering and looked away when someone needed us to stand up for them. We are haunted by the ghosts of past relationships we have broken, knowing how we've used our power to our advantage. God might love us and be calling us onward, but we don't know how to move forward with these wounds in our past weighing us down like chains and shackles. But Jesus does. This is how Paul describes it:

> In your relationships with one another, have the same mindset as Christ Jesus:
>
>> Who, being in very nature God,
>>> did not consider equality with God something to
>>> be used to his own advantage;
>> rather, he made himself nothing
>>> by taking the very nature of a servant,
>>> being made in human likeness.
>> And being found in appearance as a man,
>>> he humbled himself
>>> by becoming obedient to death— even death on a
>>> cross. (Philippians 2:5-8)

God had all the power in the world, the power that created the world. And yet when it was time to use the full measure of his power to save the world, he did so by emptying himself of it. God didn't give up his power; rather, he channeled it into powerlessness. He took on a human body made of dust. We might say God got dusty with us to mirror us. What's more, this dusty, divine human figure went even further to be impaled on a cross. He let his life be stripped away from him rather than use his power to save himself at the expense of others. He knew that if he used his power to lay down his life voluntarily, he would bring life to others.

The power of God is revealed in Jesus giving up his own life so that others might be empowered to live. Why? Because that's what powerful love does. Love never takes. Love never deceives. Love never steals or overreaches or uses others for its own advantage. Love only offers itself. It gives away. It builds others up. It forgives and restores. It speaks truth. Love makes others whole. And this kind of love never fails.

Jesus' sacrificial, self-giving love was stronger than any force that tried to kill, steal, or destroy. Our impulse to enrich ourselves by taking life from others—through gossip that steals from others' reputation, lust that steals from their bodies, moments we've hurt others to preserve ourselves, or our focus on growing our own thing so much that we've lost sight of the larger kingdom work in a city—is backlogged in our psychic systems in all kinds of ways.

But when we realize the love of Jesus is such that he'd rather be impaled to give us his life—that we don't need to take it from him but that he *wants* to give it to us—this powerful demonstration of love is so overwhelming something happens: *we are impaled too.* This is good news because it means God's power—not our own power, which has been stripped from us—will give us life. And that is a freeing place to be, even if it means we'll be walking with a limp.

As spring was approaching, our small Hope Brooklyn community had grown large enough that we couldn't meet in apartments anymore. We needed a bigger space. But space is so hard to come by in New York City, and we weren't sure what to do. I felt a new brand of fear and anxiety within me. Maybe I needed to fudge on applications or call in favors or use my power to move our church community forward in my own wisdom and power, whatever the cost.

One day in late March 2016, I was having lunch with Edwin back at Yayo's. He asked about the vision dinners we had been hosting and our plans for building the community. Our friendship had grown. We'd had tough conversations about gentrification, race dynamics, and painful moments in our pasts. I told him I didn't know how the church was going to come to be. I wasn't sure what God wanted to do in us or through us, but we were trying to listen to him and others. We were trying to be led by him, to let him invite us into the work he had already been doing in Brooklyn. And I was trying not to force my way in my own power but to trust he had the best way in mind. But it was hard.

Edwin listened and nodded. Then he said, "Russ, we have plenty of space at Next Steps. Do you want to meet here for the next season?" I was stunned. Knowing Edwin's history with guys like me, the fact that he was offering room in their church floored me.

"Edwin, that is incredibly generous. We'd love to. How much would you rent it for?"

He looked at me, confused.

"Nothing, man. We have space. You need space. We want to be generous with what we have."

I was speechless. "Why would you do that?"

He told me about when their small ragtag group began outgrowing apartments sixteen years ago. They needed a bigger place to meet, and a local Baptist congregation in Brooklyn, which operated in a building called the Baptist Temple, invited them to share space. The Temple had its own history of giving its life and love for Brooklyn—it had housed and employed Chinese immigrants in the 1920s and emancipated enslaved peoples in the 1800s.[5] As a continuation of this self-giving, sacrificial love and generosity of spirit, the congregation offered to merge their communities and give the building to Edwin and Next Steps Community Church.

"Basically, man, this is what they did for us. How can we not do it for someone else? It's what Christians do."

On that day, God wrestled with and impaled me in the form of Edwin Colon. He laid down his life in love and stripped me of any power I might use deceptively and of any questions I had about how we were to come into Brooklyn or build a church community. Through Edwin, God welcomed me into what he was doing in the church of the impaled ones in Brooklyn. We would not come to take from Brooklyn but to offer ourselves up for her.

Our prayer would not be *God, give us Brooklyn*, but rather, *God, give us* to *Brooklyn*. In a society that puts itself first, we would use whatever space or resources or time we had to give ourselves away and find, miraculously, there were always more resources for ourselves and others the next day. But before I or Hope Brooklyn could go any further, our power needed to be transformed so we could move forward, no longer tempted to steal from others to secure our own life but offering our lives to anyone who needed it and letting God secure our place in this world.

Jesus says your past has no claim on your future. Though you've used your power to enrich yourself, you are free because Jesus has wrestled with you and not overpowered you nor been overpowered by you. You thought you could deceive him and steal God's love and protection, but you can't. You can only be blessed by it—and you already have that blessing; it's been given to the whole world. He was the Impaled One who gave his life freely that you might receive it and go forward continuing to give it away to others. Like shedding a big coat on the first warm day of spring, you can walk freely. You no longer need to use your power to steal life from anyone else, because Jesus is giving his continuously to you. But like Jesus, you now have scars. Like Jacob, you now walk with a limp.

THE BLESSING OF LIMPING IN AS A GUEST

Jacob's story ends dramatically. After his hip is dislocated, we read:

The man asked him, "What is your name?"

"Jacob," he answered.

Then the man said, "Your name will no longer be Jacob, but Israel, because you have struggled with God and with humans and have overcome."

Jacob said, "Please tell me your name."

But he replied, "Why do you ask my name?" Then he blessed him there.

So Jacob called the place Peniel, saying, "It is because I saw God face to face, and yet my life was spared."

The sun rose above him as he passed Peniel, and he was limping because of his hip. (Genesis 32:27-31)

Jacob, now Israel, continues his life journey, forever limping. He can no longer overcome through his own strength, for it has been stripped from him; instead, it must be through the self-giving power and blessing of his God. As C. S. Lewis wrote, "They say of some temporal suffering, 'No future bliss can make up for it,' not knowing that Heaven, once attained, will work backward and turn even that agony into a glory."[6]

Once we no longer consider the power to take care of our lives "something to be grasped" but lay it down, becoming a sacrificial servant to others just like Jesus, the ground we walk on opens to us, inviting us into spaces we never could have found alone—as if it were waiting the whole time for us to simply ask.

When you no longer take care of yourself, you watch God begin to take care of you. And every time he does, it's a scarred reminder that this voluntary, self-giving love is the most powerful thing in the world. Just like the people in Egypt, who were given a meal to remind them of their new identity, Jacob was given a limp to remind him that this new relationship with God, epitomized by a new name, was the true blessing in life. He wouldn't be able to run as fast as before. He'd have to walk a bit slower. But whenever he was vulnerable to attack, he'd get to watch his God's power truly shine through his weakness. God would give to him so that he could give to the world.

After meeting with Edwin in the spring of 2016, we began to host Brooklyn Tables in the basement of Next Steps Community Church that summer. We would meet to cook a meal, share a brief time of teaching, and discuss. Here we were, a new church led by people just moving into the neighborhood, welcomed by those who had lived in Brooklyn most of their lives.

They welcomed us to their table so that we might welcome others to ours. JP and Edwin and Raymond and Gus and Chris and Monty and Pedro—wonderful people who made room for us, who shared with us not just the gospel but their very lives.

After the gift of our limp in Edwin, Anna and I watched God move on our behalf in the most miraculous ways. Even while meeting at Next Steps, Anna and I were still living in Queens because finding an apartment in Brooklyn was difficult and expensive. We didn't want to break the lease we had signed when I'd been the pastoral resident at Hope Astoria. Moreover, we knew Hope Brooklyn's arrangement with Edwin was temporary; it was only until we could find a more permanent home for the church. So that summer, Anna and I were praying for two permanent homes: one for Hope Brooklyn and one for us.

We walked into all sorts of places—schools, art galleries, music venues, churches—inquiring whether they would rent to our church on a more permanent basis. They all said no. But we weren't deterred because, after seeing so much, we knew God was in this. We knew it wasn't about us using our power to fight for our lives but waiting for God's self-giving power to invite us into the next chapter. We were limping along, praying, and waiting for God to show us where to go next.

One Wednesday in July, we walked into an elementary school and met the front-office staff and custodial team. They were gracious in a way that seemed out of character with New York City. When we asked about the possibility of renting space for the church ongoingly, they put the rental application into our hands and almost begged us to apply.

The next day I received a text from Kris, the pastor of Hope Astoria. He had grown up in Brooklyn and said a woman from his old church wanted me to call her. When I did, I learned that she and her husband owned a brownstone in Brooklyn. They had just been informed that their top-floor tenant was moving out. She knew of Hope Brooklyn and wanted to bless us by allowing Anna and me to rent the place if it worked out.

"What are you looking for?" she asked.

"A one bedroom," Anna replied.

"Ours is a small two."

I showed her our budget.

"We'll gladly rent it to you at that amount," the owner said. Later, I learned it was for an amount lower than market value.

Anna and I had goosebumps.

We needed to move out of our Queens apartment by October 1. The current tenant was moving out at the end of September. Uncanny. If you've ever lived in New York, you know how incredible this opportunity was. The housing market in the city is so absurdly difficult that there can be multiple applications even for a single dilapidated unit. It's such a seller's market that listings don't include the square footage because tenants don't care; they just need a place. What's more, a "broker's fee" is required for renters, meaning a real estate broker takes 10–15 percent commission of annual rent just for showing a renter the apartment so that the landlords don't have to deal with it.

Basically, it's dog-eat-dog. It feels like nearly everyone lies, cheats, backstabs, fights, and does whatever is required to secure a place and preserve their life, even if someone else gets hurt. But with the school and now this apartment, we hadn't had to do a thing. We'd just waited without working for it at all, without exerting any of our own power.

I will not let you go until you bless me. And so he blessed him.

"Where is your place?" I asked, knowing that Brooklyn, independent of the other four boroughs, was the fifth largest city in America. It was massive, and she owned one brownstone.

"On Dean and Smith," she said.

Our mouths dropped open. Our new apartment, a place we had been given without lifting a finger, was two blocks away from the school where but a few days ago we were told Hope Brooklyn could rent as our new home.

We could barely speak. It was one of those moments we still return to now, in awe of this God who enters our messes and wrestles with us. He was teaching us to wait, to listen, to come not to overpower but to receive and limp in as a guest. It's amazing how God moves for you when you can't move for yourself or when you move more slowly than others. It builds faith. It doesn't create reserves full of security. But you discover that the ground you walk is *Peniel.* You learn what it means to see God face to face and live as one truly blessed.

Four

The God at the Bottom of the Wall

O ne morning that July, I received a call that my eighty-three-year-old maternal grandfather, Papa, had died in the night. He had been battling pancreatic cancer the previous year, so our family knew it was coming. He was ready. Still, the shock of that moment was disorienting, knowing we would no longer be able to speak or laugh together.

Papa was one of seven children born to a poor German family in Lexington, North Carolina, a small textile town in the western part of the state. He was a stoic man who grew more gregarious as he got older. I remember him being emotionless when I was a boy. Not cold—emotionless but with a warm heart for his family. He taught me to love baseball and the Atlanta Braves. A star player himself, he was drafted by the St. Louis Cardinals but instead chose to enlist in the army and fight in the Korean War. When I was a boy, Papa used to comb my hair, parting it down the left side and brushing it over, just like his. Even into my young teens, Papa would comb my hair sometimes. Though he was emotionless, he loved his family. We all knew it. I hadn't seen him too often in the final years of his life, but that morning I grieved for my grandfather, and I was grateful he had lived.

The earliest manuscripts of Ephesians don't include the opening line saying it was written for the "church in Ephesus"; rather, they jump straight into the body of the letter.[1] This wasn't uncommon. However, it could mean that the theology wasn't just for one church but for multiple— maybe even all of them. So, it should make us pay a little closer attention to whatever follows. Ephesians talks a lot about how the Jews and Gentiles were now brothers and sisters in this new Christian family. This was not natural to any of them, so it did not come easily. But this was their new family. They were no longer bound by their grandparents' blood but by Jesus'.

That summer, this idea of family became reality for our new church. We were meeting twice a month at Next Steps Community Church for meals and community building. We hung twinkle lights between four beige pillars holding up the room and slapped up a tapestry of colorful tessellated triangles behind the pillars. We unrolled an orange rug, put out tablecloths, lit tea candles, and positioned fake flowers, trying to transform the basement into a living room.

Two of the first friends I made, David Santos and Josh Zepeda, had lived almost all their lives in Brooklyn. David was in his midforties, Puerto Rican, worked for Goldman Sachs's IT department, and loved motorcycles and weight-lifting. Josh was twenty-seven (my age), Honduran, born in Spanish Harlem, and now lived in Sunset Park with his wife, Christina, and their two kids, Cheyanna and Julie. He tried to convert me into a comic book fan and, along with David, geeked out over break dancing and hip-hop. Early on, we spent time talking about the history of Brooklyn, specifically the evolutions of neighborhoods. Franklin Avenue was the spot where all the new restaurants and shops were going up.

"That's where you would go to buy weed back in the day," David said.

I told them I was taking an improv class on Douglass and Nevins. Josh was amazed that this part of Brooklyn was now hosting improv classes. Carroll Gardens, now overtaken by strollers and patios, was not too long ago populated by the Italian mafia (shh—you didn't hear it from me). Josh and Dave talked about the break dancing crews of the past and how every church in the nineties seemed to have a rap troop for evangelism. Dave even had a rap name: "The Lord's Ambassador." They kept swapping stories, describing a life and a Brooklyn I never knew.

As the conversation went on, I grew embarrassed. Why in the world would they be open to being pastored by and being friends with a guy who literally shared none of their experiences growing up? We knew two different Brooklyns. How would we even come together as a new church family?

FAMILY IN-GROUPS

Our conversations revealed a double-edged sword. We all knew families are a gift. They provide comfort, love, protection, and meaning. However, as soon as we have an in-group that defines our family, we have also created its out-group. That means we are now deeply committed to maintaining our group's identity at all costs. This usually entails making sure our family is superior to the other one, even if it's only in our minds. And the things we use to demonstrate superiority are, one might say, unique. Neighborhoods, improv classes, evangelistic rap troops, how long you've lived or not lived in a place—all sorts of things. Paul describes the fight in Ephesians like this:

> Therefore, remember that formerly you who are Gentiles by birth and called "uncircumcised" by those who call themselves "the circumcision" (which is done in the body by human hands)—remember that at that time you were separate from Christ, excluded from citizenship in Israel and foreigners to the covenants of the promise, without hope and without God in the world. (Ephesians 2:11-12)

Maybe circumcision status isn't how you define your friends and enemies anymore. But this concept of believing we're superior to others because of some cultural identifier or practice, ideology, doctrine, or morality issue isn't exactly new. And it's only getting worse. Our polarized public discourse is sending us further into our respective self-justifying echo chambers. Technology allows us to curate our lives so we can airbrush our less acceptable traits and then interpret any discomfort or inconvenience as a sign of relational unhealth, or worse. The seemingly infinite niche groups on the internet give our tribalistic impulses full rein. It's so easy now to find people *just* like you, down to the specific idiosyncrasy of your taste in 1970s Parisian movies, that you don't ever have to be with people who don't act or think like you. So, the thought of having to get to know or *be family with* someone you seemingly have little in common with is the furthest thing from your experience.

What's more, as Paul alludes to, how do we do this now that the new family is composed of people we previously hated and who hated us? How is the blood of Jesus stronger than that of our grandfathers or our favorite pundit or our favorite YouTuber? It's a noble image Ephesians paints of this new family. It just seems so unrealistic in our times. And when it's so easy to create our specific in-group that we never have to stray outside of, it's just as easy to caricature the out-group and assume the absolute worst of them.

I believe we do this for a simple reason: the wounds in our souls haven't been healed. It's why confirmation bias is natural to us. We're looking for reasons to believe what we've always believed, because that feeling we may be less secure than we like, that feeling of vulnerability and helplessness, that feeling of fragile weakness that lies deep inside, is terrifying. I once heard a sentiment attributed to Dr. Martin Luther King Jr.: "We will continue to despise people until we have recognized, loved, and accepted what is despicable in ourselves."[2] Or, put another way in a quote attributed to Dr. King, "It's hard for people to live without someone to look down upon—to really look down upon. It is not just that they feel cheated out of someone to hate. *It is that they are compelled to look more closely into what they don't like within themselves.*"

Dr. King is saying that a group is often defined not by what they're *for* but who they're *against.* We pay an inordinate amount of attention to the other person's or group's flaws, which affords us the luxury of not having to deal with our own. Consequently, if we expend enough energy focusing on all that's wrong with that group over there and none on examining ourselves, we're going to believe our group is superior. And at least in our reality, it will seem undebatable! It's easier to say it's all their fault instead of doing the hard work of first asking, *In what ways do I shoulder some responsibility?* Jesus says something similar: we focus so much on a speck in our neighbor's eye that we fail to recognize the log protruding from our own.

There's the spouse who notices every one of their partner's faults but never notices that they spend hours on their phone to cope with their own emotions. There's the employee who spends all their time complaining about their dysfunctional organization and none on trying to make it better. There's the Christian who writes a book about their church's hypocrisy but doesn't include even a paragraph about their own.

Of course, I'm not talking about *you*. I'm talking about *me*. I transfer my fear, brokenness, and inner wounds onto *them*, pass judgment, wash my hands of their blood, and tell myself that's why I am morally, religiously, and materially right, more trustworthy, more enlightened, and more worthy of love.

We all do it. Whether Jew or Gentile, no matter what race, nation, or political party, we assume the brokenness is *their* fault and if they would just get their act together and take out that speck, we'd be in a better world. But before we even give them a chance to change, we eviscerate them in our hearts. We sacrifice them—through gossip and slander, a scathing and uncharitable Twitter post, outright canceling, or even just a lack of empathy—and give our group another night of self-righteous sleep.

Why do we do it? Because deep down we know how vulnerable we really are. We know our souls are riddled with mortal wounds, and we're bleeding badly. We haven't addressed what we despise in ourselves. I had a fast-paced friend, a district attorney, tell me that he was afraid of slowing down. When I asked him why, he answered jokingly, "Then I'd have to live with myself."

But it wasn't a joke. Isn't it easier to not deal with your own wounds by focusing on the wounds of others? Isn't it easier to not deal with your own pain by obsessing over those not dealing with theirs? Isn't it easier to live with yourself when you're too busy going after the bad(der) guys?

THE TRUE VICTIM, A FINAL SACRIFICE

On the night Papa died, a group of us met at a local café on a beautiful summer evening. We were still a burgeoning community made up of people who were from Brooklyn and those who were not. There were people of various nationalities, ethnicities, and socioeconomic positions present. Men and women, older and younger, Republican and Democrat . . . it really was a special and horrendously difficult group because vastly different histories and perspectives were all taking up space in our new family.

Josh brought his daughter, Julie, and Dave came with his motorcycle helmet in hand, a line of sweat on his brow. The evening was particularly intense. Though Papa's death was weighing on me, I knew everyone was experiencing varying levels of pain and confusion due to disagreements at work, divisive relationships at home, social unrest, and even national conversations around race relations and upcoming elections fraught with differing opinions. It was bringing up some natural differences between us, making it difficult for us to trust one another. Everyone's legitimate pain was strong, and our conversations were heated. It seemed easier to defend our innocence and retreat to our side rather than listen to see if others had any wisdom to share or insight to offer.

While listening, I watched Josh and Julie playing off to the side; he'd throw her into the air and catch her. They both looked happy. Julie laughed with complete trust her father would catch her every time. Her figure was silhouetted by the string lights puncturing the dark blue sky above. Mourning the loss of Papa in my heart, I found the scene so beautiful during a very stressful moment.

As I listened to our new church family's heated conversation, thinking of my grandfather and watching a dad and his daughter play off to the side, the thought struck me: *What if we start there?* With our wounded hearts and obstructed vision, we find it easier to focus on the other side's faults and flaws, caricaturing them and reducing their humanity to a monstrous image. But what if we instead choose to focus on how they may be just like us? Fathers and daughters, mothers and sons, grandparents, cousins, nephews, and nieces who eat like us, pray like us, play games, and celebrate holidays. Sure, maybe one side is circumcised and the other isn't. But they both care about passing on an identity of love and respect to their children. Before we rush to pull out the obstructions from one another's eyes, what if we take the time to confess that we're all a little blind?

If our nature finds it easier to identify what's despicable in others and use that as a reason to sacrifice them, there's something else we all have in common. *We know what it's like to feel loss. We know what it's like to grieve.* What if our first step toward coming together as a new family is shared grief—corporate lament? Can we recognize, regardless of why we're fighting, that families are being destroyed? Even though debate and reform are good gifts of God, before we rush to explain why our group is the victim and sacrifice the other side, can we first pause and mourn the blood flowing in the street together? Can we grieve that we're the kind of people who would sacrifice strangers rather than deal with our own woundedness? Can we sit humbly and weep over the fact that fathers will no longer toss their children into the air and that children will no longer believe they can fly?

This is what Paul explains in Ephesians. He levels a conversation that is going nowhere by declaring that circumcision and uncircumcision make no difference in God's eyes. All the ways that Jews and Gentiles have persecuted each other in regard to this situation have no bearing on God's family. To prove it, God goes a step further. He takes on a form that all of them will understand and be humbled by: the sacrificial victim.

> But now in Christ Jesus you who once were far away have been brought near by the blood of Christ.
>
> For he himself is our peace, who has made the two groups one and has destroyed the barrier, the dividing wall of hostility, by setting aside in his flesh the law with its commands and regulations. His purpose was to create in himself one new humanity out of the two, thus making peace, and in one body to reconcile both

of them to God through the cross, by which he put to death their hostility. (Ephesians 2:13-16)

While we're focusing on our differences and sacrificing others in our hearts to feel safe behind our own walls, God wants us to know that he sees no difference between us. We all act the same way. We all know what it's like to be a victim of something unjust, and we all have a little bit of the villain inside us too. We're equally deserving (or undeserving) of life, equally part of the same poorly mirroring human family, equally bleeding out from a wounded world because we're wounded inside and wounding each other on the outside.

But we struggle to admit that. It's *her* fault that I can't trust anymore. It's *their* fault that our society is broken. It's never *my* fault—if we say those words out loud, we fear we will be overwhelmed by deep, dark, vulnerable sadness and won't be able to trust others with it. It's as T. S. Eliot wrote in his poem "The Rock": "They constantly try to escape / from the darkness outside and within / by dreaming of systems so perfect that no one will / need to be good."[3] It's not that systems can't be improved. They unequivocally can, and the Bible demonstrates they should be. It's just a matter of where we *start*. Before we can escape the darkness out there, we must escape the darkness in here. Before we can help remove the speck from our neighbor's eye, the log we despise must go from our own.

If God is the only one who sees clearly, the only one without wounds, and the only one with enough courage to meet us as we are, how does he tell us that all this fighting and sacrificing is nonsense distracting us from the deeper reality that he is with us in our grieving woundedness, loves us where we are, and longs to bring us into one family again? While we are all sacrificing the other side and refusing to look within, God says, "I'll become the other side. I'll become your sacrificial victim and force you to really see yourself."

Because it's not just any flesh and blood Paul references; it's *crucified* flesh and blood. It's not that God united us through a human body but through an *executed human body*. God came as Jesus not to climb up the wall of our judgments and hostilities that separate us but to climb down it and dismantle it from the foundation. He came not to justify himself but to pour himself out. He came not to tell us it's our fault (which, let's be real, it is), but to tell us he loves us and will fix it. He came to mirror the real us. He had every right in the world to condemn us—there was no speck in his eye; he saw things clearly. Yet he did not use that right. Instead, he let us believe *we* were right and let us kill him. But since he has now embodied the true victim of the world unjustly killed, our fate is in his hands. We all literally owe him our lives.

And what does he do once the Jews and Gentiles realize their lives are up to him? He says, "Now that you're listening, hear this: you can no longer take out your anger and fear on one another because it's already been taken out on me. You are the same: in your fear and violence, you both put me to death. The whole world put me to death. Rome neglected justice. Israel did away with truth. My disciples abandoned me. One of them betrayed me. Everyone has wronged me. And I'm forgiving all of you. That means you have something in common."

God became the true and final victim. He said that life is found when we stop looking down on others—whether we're right, partly right, mostly right, or completely wrong—and instead come down the wall and join him at the bottom. If we're all at the bottom of the wall facing our inner wounds, knowing God is giving us life even though we deserve death, then we don't even need a wall anymore because we no longer have to protect ourselves. We're all going to live regardless of what we may deserve. We can become a new family now.

Circumcised or noncircumcised, original Brooklynite or new, we gather around our shared grief from being a people that puts others to death to avoid our own woundedness, so that our hearts of fear and violence can begin to be emptied by his forgiveness. It's how he removes the log from our eyes so that we can see each other a little more clearly, a little more like how he sees us.

Over the next few weeks, Josh, Dave, and I continued the conversation that had begun that evening in July. It's not that we saw things differently. We really didn't. It's just that we came into the conversation from different places in life, which gave us different perspectives. Then for whatever reason, probably because we were so emotionally wiped that summer, we began to vulnerably open up to one another. We revealed to each other our wounds within, our grief, what we despised, and how we longed to be healed.

I told them about Papa's death, my insecurity about leading a church when I wasn't from this city, and how deep down I believed myself to be unlovable and worthy of rejection due to my broken face. Dave told us about how a painful season of loss in his life impacted his faith and self-perception. Josh confessed he felt constantly overlooked in his youth and shared how that affected the way he saw himself and others.

The three of us shared stories about our experiences with racism, fear, and grace. God moved among us; we cried; we prayed. And when we rose that summer, we discovered a stronger foundation for a new church family, something that all of us can achieve. That's the gift and the *true* sacrifice of those who want to follow Jesus. We must give up whatever we use to protect ourselves and vulnerably meet at the bottom of the wall with Jesus. We must trust that the family we're entering there—the one that is built on receiving God's forgiveness in a world that sacrifices others to protect itself—is stronger than the family we're leaving behind. That a family bound by their willingness to face what's despicable on the inside is a family resilient and humble enough to engage with what's despicable on the outside too. In a small way, we began to build out this family that summer—one where all of us came face to face.

And when our souls drew closer to one another, our eyes a little clearer, I saw for the first time that all our faces were severely scarred—no matter what color. It's not that the color wasn't important; it very much was. But it was our scars that brought us together, affording us the grace to learn more about the histories found in our faces and those of our grandfathers.

A HOUSE OF MURDERERS WITH A SHARED TASK

In the end, we found ourselves defenseless with each other but no longer vulnerable. At the bottom of the wall, we realized there was one final task Paul gave us in Ephesians to epitomize the next stage of the new family's journey: to help build Jesus' house.

> Consequently, you are no longer foreigners and strangers, but fellow citizens with God's people and also members of his household, built on the foundation of the apostles and prophets, with Christ Jesus himself as the chief cornerstone. In him the whole building is joined together and rises to become a holy temple in the Lord. And in him you too are being built together to become a dwelling in which God lives by his Spirit. (Ephesians 2:19-22)

In essence, if you want to see where a family's heart really resides, look at the structures it builds. The cornerstone establishes the foundation, and the foundation charts the direction of the entire thing. If Jesus is the cornerstone of our new family, then the foundation of our house, the church, is his love inside our murderous and grieving natures. His grace for our wounds within will be our cement and mortar for the whole thing. And out of that deep peace in our hearts, we can begin to build a reconciled family for all his people. To reconcile something is to join what was previously broken, to stitch it back together, to make a scar.

We will know if the wounds of Jesus' people are healed by the types of churches and tables they build. If our Sunday mornings actively omit the presence of another group through class, politics, race, or something else, then the foundation of our church is still not built from the bottom of the wall like Ephesians describes. If your friend group is keeping out a certain type of person, perhaps there's still a wall in your heart separating you from them rather than a scar of reconciliation. This is ironic, as scholar Larry Hurtado contends that one of the unique features of the first church was that, from the start, it was multiracial, multiethnic, and comprised of all socioeconomic classes: "That is, from this early point onward, early Christian religious identity was not tied to one's ethnicity and did not involve a connection to any particular group."[4]

Those in the house of God were appealing to a deeper foundation than their prior nationalism, politics, class, or identity. They were appealing to the peace spoken to them in their woundedness by Jesus. They had no need to cut others down to feel superior, nor did they need to defend themselves. They no longer felt compelled to call out other people's specks, because their own planks were gone. They were free and able to listen, learn from, and help people, even if they were indicted by what others said. Then they were free to ask for forgiveness and work to make amends. They were free to build a new family, a new house, a new world by stitching things back together, by teaching one another to find each other in their scars, because that's where Jesus found them.

I think that's why Jesus left the sharing of a meal for his disciples as the new family's primary activity. Not only does it reinforce the interception of our identities, but it also reminds us of our shared task to stitch back together all things and all people as Jesus has stitched us back together with God. And it starts one meal at a time. At the table we sit across from people we don't know, or even people we thought we knew but whose deeper stories we didn't know: their rejection, their abandonment issues, their fears, and their failures—the same stuff we all wrestle with.

In the Catholic tradition, the bread is called the "host." It derives from the Latin *hostia*, meaning "sacrificial victim." Which means when we, the new family, meet to offer bread and wine with Jesus, we offer him up as our sacrificial victim, and then we receive him too. "We consume the very same thing that we offer," writes Professor Tom Boylston.[5] We acknowledge that we're the kind of people who would put Jesus, and one another, to death. We confess that we've met Jesus and he forgave us, for we did not know what we were doing. So we all sit down to break bread. And in our complexity, sorrow, joy, suffering, confusion, and anger, we have time to figure it out because we're all murderers and all pardoned, and Jesus' scars shine forth from the bread, the cup, and our own smiling faces. That's a strong family.

That summer, Josh and Christina dedicated Julie to God. She was the first child dedication at Hope Brooklyn. They invited all their family and cooked us a delicious meal. There was creamy yellow rice, charred grilled chicken, steaming black beans, and warm tortillas. Josh read a beautiful prayer he wrote for Julie about the type of family he wanted her to grow up in.

He ended by praying she would grow into a woman who did not know fear. As he prayed, I thought of Papa. I had just returned from his funeral. It was good to see extended family since there weren't many occasions for us all to get together anymore. But being with Hope Brooklyn that night, dedicating a new child to our growing church family, and sharing a meal, I realized that this, too, was my family.

Josh and Christina, Dave and Marisol, Nathan and Stephanie. So many of us from so many places—male and female, every color, from Brooklyn and not. This night we were all welcoming a new niece into our midst because in our woundedness, Jesus had met us and spoken peace to us there. We began our church family around the table. We would soon move into our new home at the school and forgo the twinkle lights and tablecloths, but the meal was the same even as we grew. We always ate together, scarred face to scarred face.

Seemingly overnight, Julie was five. Once during service, she came up with Josh for Communion and took a piece of bread. She plunged her entire hand into the cup, pulling it out and dripping purple stains onto the rugs. Everyone laughed, yet she should've been the one laughing at us because she was teaching us a lesson. In this house, we don't take a sip of grace. We plunge our entire souls into that cup of life. We don't go one step at a time. We fly into the air, our hair dancing free in the wind. We have huge grins on our faces and laughter in our hearts before we start freefalling to the bottom of the wall.

Because every time we taste the wine and bread, our Father is catching us in his arms before launching us back into the air. It's how we'll trust the peace spoken to our souls. It's how we'll learn to gaze up and watch the clouds pass by. It's how we'll grow to not know fear.

Five

The God Whose Rib Makes Us Whole

Among life's certainties is that nothing stays the same. If we find a swath of peace, the tranquility will soon be broken. If we finally accept our wounds as a way—*the way*—Jesus loves us most deeply, we will soon forget that lesson. And if we have a spouse journeying beside us as we learn this lesson over and over, the covenant will become a crucible before long.

At the time we got married, Anna and I had never had a fight. We had been "annoyed" with each other, but we always got over it. We focused too much on why we loved the other person—or why we feared losing them—to make them angry or defensive and endanger the relationship.

We had met in Portland, Oregon, while I was an intern at her church. From the start, we'd had a connection that was different from anything we'd felt before. Our stories weirdly meshed. For example, her dad, born two years before the polio vaccine, had contracted polio as an infant. He had lived his entire life with a weak leg. So the first man Anna ever loved was a man with very visible imperfections. When she met me and saw my face scarred from my congenital disorder, it was not hard for her to love me. It fit her experience.

We enjoyed hiking together, and we would often break into random voices. "Look at that moss creepin' up that tree!" I'd shout in a Scottish inflection.

"Oh yes, the moss is a'creepin'!" she'd shout back.

It was odd, to be sure, but it was us, effortlessly. We had the same taste in music (Bon Iver to feel sad; Lumineers to fall in love; JLo when we wanted to dance), the same ideas of fun (walking, board games, animal videos dubbed over with human voices), and even a similar disposition toward theological topics (I could riff longer, but she always dropped the mic).

We were married in January 2015, eighteen months after meeting and nine months before moving to New York City. Our wedding took place on a cold, drizzly Saturday. Standing before the oversized window of an old warehouse underneath a beautiful, lush floral piece, we promised to be there for each other no matter what came our way. It was true and honest—as honest as it could be. We always had a sign-off when one of us would leave the other for a bit. One would say, "Only you, only yours," to which the other would respond, "Forever and always." On our wedding day, these two mantras bound themselves together. Through our vows we fused our lives, stating that it would only be the two of us, exclusively, in mind, body, and spirit. Our bond would be eternal and without end.

Fast forward eighteen months to the summer of 2016 when we were at Next Steps Community Church hosting Brooklyn Table. We were making friends, building community, and still commuting between Queens and Brooklyn. Anna and I had just gotten our apartment, and we knew Hope Brooklyn was moving into the school later that fall. Anna had also started a cinematography company, for which I became her second shooter since we couldn't afford to hire other contractors. The church was pushing uphill. Both ventures were in full-on growth mode. We were out six nights a week meeting people. Weekends were consumed with filming weddings on Saturday and gathering as a church community on Sunday.

In these eighteen months of living together for the first time, Anna and I started to have some fights. Like, *real* ones.

We were forthright in telling the other how they annoyed us, usually without them asking. It was always the smallest things—Anna not running water on her dishes, me asking a question twice, Anna not saving a particular receipt, me asking the wrong question (you'll notice some themes).

Our respective focuses had shifted. While we meshed in some ways, we learned that we glaringly did not in others. The cute Scottish accents were replaced with cutting remarks. We hadn't hiked in forever. And we no longer said, "Only you, only yours," followed sweetly by, "Forever and always." In short, we were not enjoying our relationship.

Sometimes, we'd think back to our wedding and wonder *who were we?* and *what were we thinking when we made those vows? Forever and always? Like forever* and *always?* There was so much we didn't know about ourselves, about the other person, about relationships. We were not alike as much as we thought we were or had hoped to be.

Here's the confusing part: that summer of 2016, we were just as honest as the day of our wedding. Only now we had more data to go on about ourselves, the other person, and ourselves in relation to the other person. The new data prompted a new interpretation—namely, that we were not so sure we were appropriately matched. Who was right—the Anna and Russell who knew they loved each other more than anyone else or the Anna and Russell who couldn't muster the smallest amount of grace toward each other? Because we were truthful in both seasons. And while we were quick to see how the other person wounded us, we weren't as adept at noticing how we wounded the other—or noticing our own wounds, period.

Isn't that the conundrum in relationships? The first year it's all daises and rainbows. But in time, we get a whiff of gasoline and see someone a little tempted to strike a match. We learn more information about the other person and ourselves. Shoot, we change. Life changes us. And even the best of us have unhealed wounds exacerbated by the brokenness of the world. Meanwhile, we're supposed to process all this while our person is brushing their teeth beside us wearing old, tattered pajamas, hasn't showered, and bought the wrong type of flour for the tenth time at the grocery store even though we explicitly asked them to pay closer attention.

This just seems like it's all set up to frustrate us. What is God up to?

THE FIRST TIME GOD SAYS
SOMETHING IS NOT GOOD

In the story of Genesis, we watch God's creation emerge in its place right on time. On the sixth day of God's enterprise, we read of the making of the *adam*. I write it that way because the Hebrew language has some distinctions that will become important in the story. But the *adam* is a much broader word in Hebrew than just the English name "Adam." It's probably better translated "the human."

God makes the human and puts him in the garden with directions for how to plant blueberry bushes and feed the wildebeest. Very cute. A perfectly balanced creation so far. But then in a staggering statement God makes a confession: "The LORD God said, 'It is not good for the man to be alone. I will make a helper suitable for him'" (Genesis 2:18). This is the first time in the creative masterpiece that God has said something is not good. Light is good. The sun and moon are good. Birds and fish and animals are good. The human is very good. But the human being alone? This is not good at all.

It's naive to suggest God made a mistake that he then rectified. I do wonder, though, how the omniscient Creator didn't foresee this complication. We can speculate all we want. But for whatever reason, there is now something *not good* in the cosmos. The human is alone. And we're all waiting to see what God does next.

There was a 2017 *New Yorker* article called "Why Facts Don't Change our Minds," in which cognitive scientists made the case that our strongest advantage over other species is our ability to cooperate.[1] It's all because humans are really good at, and desperately crave, bonding together and protecting those bonds. The key idea is simple—more than we crave what is true, we crave love and relationship. *We don't want to be alone. It's not good for us to be alone.*

Moreover, there's an imperiling trend in the Western world right now: rising rates of chronic loneliness. It was declared a public health emergency and an epidemic in many countries even before the Covid-19 shutdowns and quarantined lives we all suffered. Studies have shown how loneliness affects the human body, and the results are shocking. In one study, it was discovered that social exclusion works on the same part of the brain as physical pain—meaning social pain *feels* just like physical pain.[2] It's been found that lonelier people are at greater risk for cardiovascular disease, cancer, and respiratory illness, and some researchers have said that chronic, debilitating loneliness is akin to smoking fifteen cigarettes a day![3]

But this aloneness is not cured by simply having friends or being in a room full of people. New York, one of the most densely populated cities, is one of the loneliest. How can that be? Because we need to not only be proximate with other humans but to share our lives with them. It's not just the connection but the *depth* of connection.

This is the major issue with social media sites, as described by Sherry Turkle in her book *Alone Together*. She describes how "without the demands and rewards of intimacy and empathy, we end up feeling alone while together online."[4] The high of connecting online comes to a crashing halt the first time we meet for dinner and a conversation. For true relationship to flourish—for true bonds to be formed so people do not feel alone—people need to share physical, mental, emotional, and spiritual resources.

All this data points in only one direction: relationships are so deeply intertwined with what it means to be human that our bodies are affected by the presence or absence of such bonds. Our life, or early death, is literally predicated on the depth of connections we have with others. Science has proven what God already said—*it is not good for us to be alone*. There must be something deeper in the connection that tethers people together such that their lives would be missing something vital, like a body missing a limb, if the connection were broken.

Reciprocity. That's the key word. Loneliness is counteracted through reciprocity. We want a mutually giving relationship in which our life is tied up with another person's life. We want another person's life to give our life a reason to continue, and vice versa.

The question is, where do we find that?

In our society, there are two competing narratives trying to answer this. The church says that the wound of our aloneness is fixed within marriage: do not give yourself to another until you find your soulmate, and then you will not be alone. Our society says, "Find someone who fulfills you, or find a new person whenever the aloneness comes back." But as we discover, neither works. We're still alone in marriage, and going from partner to partner is draining. We search online for real connection and come up for air, asphyxiated and lost. Our hearts ache with aloneness.

Science and Scripture reveal "it is not good," yet we have no idea how to make "it"—the aloneness—go away. The loneliest day of all is when we wake up next to our spouse, or visit our friend, or have that conversation with our sibling and realize we don't know who they are because of how they've wounded us, or we don't know ourselves because of how we wounded *them*, or a combination of both. Either way, we realize that this person we put so much hope in to deal with our wounded, lonely soul has failed us. And be it a spouse, a friend, a sibling, or a parent, that is a hopeless feeling to which we can all relate.

THE GOD WHO IS RELATIONSHIP

One of the tougher parts to stomach in our predicament is that our Creator has never been alone on a Friday night. Two of the key foundations in our knowledge of God is that he is *simple* and he is *triune*. When we say *God*, we don't mean some spiritual being in the sky with wrinkles, a beard, and the type of forearms a guy would kill for. Rather, "God is not one Being among others . . . but the very *Ground of Being* itself."[5] We're not talking about one form of existence but the *root*, the *source* of existence. It is as Paul told the Athenians in Acts 17—God is the one in whom we live and move and have our being. This is how Augustine prays: "God, you are more in me than I am in me." God is deeper in your bones and your lungs than is that silly little voice in your head you call consciousness. We are from God, of God, moving toward God. There is nothing beyond him, nothing to divide into him. God is the simplest source of Being from whom everything has emerged.

But that's not all God is either. God is *triune*. Which means the simple, indivisible ground of all Being is actually three persons. One of the more important documents for learning about God is the Nicene Creed. It was written in AD 325 to quite the fanfare. For our purposes, there's a significant line about how we believe there is one simple God that exists in three unique persons—Father, Son, and Holy Spirit. When the creed references Jesus, the human who walked the earth and showed us a life lived in perfect relationship with God, there's this infamous line that a lot of ink was spilled over in the fourth century: "Jesus is light of light, true God from true God, begotten not made, of the same substance as the Father."

What was the church trying to get at? I think this: the root of our existence is *relationship*. God is complete and eternal reciprocity. God is not Father, Son, *and* Holy Spirit but Father-Son-Holy Spirit. It'd be like a child asking her mom and dad where she came from. Who is more fundamental to the child's existence—the mother or the father? The child emerged not from the father, nor from the mother, but from *father-mother*. The ground of the child's existence is the relationship shared between father-mother. It's a staggering thought. And it makes a lot of sense the more we consider why we are so wounded by our aloneness and why we crave love more than we crave truth. Because the truth of God is love! The deep substance of God's being is his relationship. God is not alone and has never been alone. There is no aloneness in God. Which is why God says, looking at the human on that sixth day of creation, it's not good for us to be alone either.

EZER KENEGDO'S IMPOSSIBLE TASK

After God says it's not good for the human to be alone, he says, "I will make a *helper* suitable for him" (Genesis 2:18, emphasis mine). An *ezer kenegdo*. The word has been translated all sorts of ways throughout history, but broken down, *ezer* means strength, power, and salvation.[6] Interestingly, in most other cases, it is God who is called Israel's *ezer*. *Kenegdo* is a compound word that means "according to the sight of him." To be *kenegdo* is to reciprocate someone, to correspond to them in power and likeness, to *mirror* them. So, we could say that the *ezer kenegdo* is a savior who reciprocates and mirrors the human. It is a power equal in power and a likeness equal in likeness. We might say the *ezer kenegdo* is *true human of true human, begotten not made, of the same substance as the human.* But the issue is that we don't know where to find them.

Right after God says he will make for the human a saving helper, it is written, "So the human gave names to all the livestock, the birds in the sky and all the wild animals. But for the human no suitable *ezer kenegdo* was found" (Genesis 2:20 author's paraphrase).

Martin Buber, a Jewish philosopher, wrote a famous book titled *I-Thou*. The book is dense, but the idea is simple. We have two types of relationships in this world: I-It and I-Thou. I-It is characterized by possessing power over someone such that "it" exists to serve "I." When God tells Adam to name the animals, he's facilitating I-It relationships because Adam has power over the animals. Interestingly, the first way we try to heal the wound of our aloneness is by giving others different names. We force people to be what we think we need, placing the full weight of our need for a savior onto their frail shoulders. Inevitably, they fail. "Tell us the truth, but now give us grace! Hold me accountable, but don't tell me what to do! I need you to speak up at the right time, but also make sure you always say the right things and know when I need you to simply be quiet." On and on it goes. We try to name them by demanding they do precisely what we need at every moment of our lives. It never works because *relationship is reciprocity*, and I-It relationships are never reciprocal. They are one-directional. We name people different things to try to get them to reciprocate us perfectly, but among those names, no *ezer kenegdo* is found.

This is what happened with Anna and me. When we started to feel stressed, all the things that had drawn us to the other were still there but were now offering a different interpretation. Anna's spontaneity was also her difficulty to follow through on commitments. My self-discipline could also look like micromanagement. I was anxious and insecure that Hope Brooklyn would die before it was ever born. I also felt alone and scared at just how much my sense of worth was tied to the church. When I got home, I would go to Anna, my *ezer kenegdo*. In those moments I needed her to make me feel "not alone" and to be my affirmer, my validator. But she never said the right thing. She couldn't reciprocate me how I needed. And, of course, vice versa; I could play this game too, perhaps better than Anna. She missed Portland and was struggling with the difficulty of starting a company in a city that ran faster than what she was used to. She needed me to give her back rubs and hold her hand and soothe her and encourage her. And I was failing at it.

It got worse.

"Anna, that was a selfish thing to say."

"Russell, that was a selfish thing to do."

"Anna, why won't you open up to me?"

"Russell, why won't you pursue me?"

Have you had relationships like these? When you get frustrated over your spouse or friend or parent's inability to listen and internalize what you really need from them? Or vice versa: you find yourself in another conversation about how you communicated disrespect and really wounded someone when you forgot to do that one thing. And then your own frustration boils over, and you say things and immediately recoil because you can't believe you just said that, but you're not going to be the first to apologize. It's all so tragic and sad. You're both needing each other to mirror one another's needs and make the wounded aloneness go away, but no one can do it right. You genuinely try, but you just can't be what the other person needs you to be. You aren't strong enough. Neither are they. How lonely it all is. How futilely repetitive and exhausting.

So for us, as that summer turned into fall turned into winter, our souls grew wearier, our eyes dimmer, and our love fainter.

A STRANGE SURGERY

"So the LORD God caused the man [*adam*] to fall into a deep sleep" (Genesis 2:21).

Passions fade. Anger gives way to sadness, which gives way to apathy. A point comes where you simply don't care anymore; it hurts too much to care. You just can't find that savior in your life, so you stop putting all your hope into the search. Or the person is so clearly not your savior that you're no longer expecting them to be. They're so bad at reciprocating that you don't even try to force them into it, which means you're not forcing names on them and wounding them further. Maybe, depending on what type of season you're in, you're starting to love them for who they are. That is to say, you're offering grace. But before that even comes, there is a deep, dark weariness. Your soul falls asleep.

For us, that was Christmas 2016 in Portland. That fall had kicked our butts. Some great things had happened, but we had pushed too hard. We had worked ourselves to the bone. And we had left no time for one another yet expected the other to reciprocate us instantaneously when we needed it. Like trying to wring out a dry sponge, we were both cracked and disintegrating, walking rigor mortis. We didn't have sex that entire trip. Not because we were withholding from each other; we just had no desire to ask or to apologize. Anna spent a lot of time with her friends and sisters, and I spent a lot of time with old friends and myself, which was fine. We were done.

That Christmas, like the *adam*, we fell into a deep sleep. Perhaps on this route to discovering the true Savior, we must first name one another to realize the names don't stick. Then we must despair of this and battle it out with each other or ourselves. But finally, when the night is darkest and stillest before the dawn, God puts us to sleep so he can touch the wound of our aloneness and reveal the power of the real *ezer kenegdo,* the true meaning of being made in God's image, the image of perfect relationship.

One day that Christmas holiday, I was walking my in-laws' large backyard while Anna was out with friends. I was emotionally numb, but the space we had taken from each other had given my heart time to thaw a bit. For whatever reason, I was attempting to walk a straight line back and forth across the long, grassy yard. There was something in the slow, methodical pacing from one end to the other that felt akin to meditation. I wasn't praying. But I was thinking of God. I was smoking my tobacco pipe, and the slow pace and rhythmic puffing was calming me. I kept altering my eye line from the thick grass where my feet tamped down the green blades to the gray, soggy sky above. And when I stared at the sky, I would lose my balance because the gray was impenetrable and endless and seemed to flow together like one long, insufferable substance.

Toward the back of the yard to one side was a giant tree. As I walked my lines, I edged closer to it, knowing at some point it would be in my way and I'd have to figure out what to do about it. Would I walk around it? Would I stop and turn back? Would it move for me? I kept walking, thinking, puffing. The moment arrived, and I found myself approaching the tree with a confrontation before me. As I slowly walked a good hundred steps, I didn't watch the grass or the sky but instead stared directly at the tree. It was a medium-sized evergreen with drooping needles and numerous branches that resembled weak hair. The branches were shaped like a parabola, as if lamenting their initial downward slope and suddenly deciding to make a U-turn and reach for the heavens. The tree stood there, quite still. It did not move; it did not sway; it did not seem to care for me at all. It just *was*.

And all at once, realizing how foolish this will sound, I began to get emotional. At the time, displays of emotion were rare for me, so I knew something was happening. Water filled the sponge of my soul; I soaked it up and cried it out.

Though I couldn't communicate with Anna at the moment, it felt like God was communicating with me—yes, through a tree. I know how strange that sounds. But it is what it is; you can work out if I'm crazy later. The tree that stood there, not coming after me but also not backing away, *comforted* me. God, it seemed, was there—not coming after me, not backing away. He just *was*. He had been there many years before I showed up on the earth, and he'd be there many years after I died. He had been there at the altar when Anna and I could see no wrong in each other, and he was there now when we could see no right. Suddenly, I knew God saw me and his presence was the only thing that mattered. And when I realized this, I also knew that I was happy and fortunate to be married to Anna and that we were going to be okay.

The presence of the tree signaled that there are firm, unshakable things in this world. There are deep roots, unseen in our very souls, that stretch beneath the conscious voice in our minds, the weakness of our flesh, the wounded aloneness of our soul, and the house where we sleep silently next to a spouse whose skin we've forgotten to touch but who we've pledged ourselves to for the rest of our days.

All will be well. Her name is Anna. Your name is Russell. And you are held by the ezer kenegdo *that is a stronger savior than either of you can even begin to know.*

THE RIB OF GOD AND OUR TRUE *EZER KENEGDO*

After God caused the human (*adam*) to fall into a deep sleep, he took a rib from him, which is interesting because God had been making creatures from dust. He fashioned the rib into another human, but this one was a little different. He then brought her to the first human, who exclaimed (perhaps in a Scottish accent), "This is now bone of my bones and flesh of my flesh; she shall be called 'woman,' for she was taken out of man" (Genesis 2:23).

Until now, I've belabored the point that the Hebrew word for "the human" is *adam*. And the human is looking for its *ezer kenegdo*—its savior who can reciprocate it, to no avail. But here, when presented with the creature that is formed from the rib of the human, the same material, *light of light, true human of true human, begotten not made, of the same sub-stance,* the human says, "This is it! She shall be called woman for out of man this one was taken." This is the first time in the story the human is called *ish,* which is the Hebrew word for *man.* The point is subtle but important: only after seeing the woman does the human know her as woman (*ishah*) and discover his own name as man. *The man doesn't just name the woman; the woman also names the man.* Martin Buber would call this relationship I-Thou.

When I name an "it," I acknowledge I am not the same as it. I am not of the same substance. But when I see and sur-render to "thou," I realize that my life is tied up in your life, that there is no *me* without *you,* that there is no world but the world that encounters us, and that striving and seeking salvation in another person is futile. For my salvation is not in *you,* nor in *me,* but in relationship. And in that, I dis-cover what it means to be made in the image of God—Relationship himself.

Being made in God's image is found not only in the trinitarian titles but in that invisible, hyphenated bond that makes the three persons one indivisible being. Perhaps that's why God used a rib from the man to make the woman: a rib looks like a hyphen. A shared rib is reciprocity. A shared rib is a shared life. And only Relationship himself knows how to create that.

You could read to this point and conclude that marriage is how we discover the image of God in our lives. Marriage is the pathway toward healing our wounded aloneness. While much of modern evangelicalism has espoused this theology, it's wrong. Because this is not the last time we read this story of God curing our aloneness by establishing a reciprocal relationship. In fact, the apostle Paul, who was single, refers to it in the letter of Ephesians when he's giving marriage advice to couples:

> In this same way, husbands ought to love their wives as their own bodies. He who loves his wife loves himself. After all, no one ever hated their own body, but they feed and care for their body, just as Christ does the church—for we are members of his body. "For this reason a man will leave his father and mother and be united to his wife, and the two will become one flesh." This is a profound mystery—but I am talking about Christ and the church. (Ephesians 5:28-32)

Basically, Paul is saying that marriage is an icon, not an idol.[7] An icon is meant to be looked at to lead us to the more beautiful and final version of something. So, the Genesis story of the man and woman finding a reciprocal union is an icon that leads us to our *true and final union with Jesus Christ.*

We could say that Jesus Christ is our true *ezer kenegdo.*

Jesus is the one who reciprocates us perfectly and makes us "not alone." For if Jesus is of the same substance as God, perhaps when God decided to make a covenant with humanity, God took a rib from himself—and the Son came to earth to share his life with whoever joins into loving relationship with him so that they will be shaped into the very substance of God too.

The wound of our aloneness is healed and becomes a scar when we realize it's not marriage or our spouse that is our savior reciprocating us—it's Jesus. It's not which of our friends makes us less alone, it's Jesus' friendship. And when we're his first, whether we choose marriage or remain single, we still have the same one-flesh union with Christ taking away our aloneness. Anna couldn't make me less alone. Jesus could. And when I understood that, I had more of heaven's life to give to the covenant with Anna, while she had more of the same to give to me. *All will be well. Her name is Anna. Your name is Russell. And you are held by the* ezer kenegdo *that is a stronger Savior than either of you can even begin to know.*

A WALTZ OF WOUNDEDNESS

Christmas break ended, and we arrived back in Brooklyn. Our Christmas tree was dead after going unwatered. Hope Brooklyn had a preview service the following Sunday. It was a cold, rainy January day, and the turnout was not great. Anna had tons of promising things to say. Though I tried to will myself to see what she was saying, I felt defeated. She knew that. Toward the end of that Sunday night we cuddled on our couch, which we hadn't done in a while, and watched the pilot for a new show called *This Is Us*.

We are notoriously difficult people to please in terms of TV, but this pilot blew us away. The show moves between a few characters' storylines: a husband and wife who are about to give birth to triplets, a man searching for his father who abandoned him at birth, and a pair of twins struggling to separate from each other, strike out on their own, and be adults. The commonality is that the twins, the man looking for his father, and the man whose wife is about to have triplets are all celebrating their thirty-sixth birthdays.

Sadly, the husband and wife having triplets lose one of their babies. It's crushing. But as the episode ends, we learn that a newborn baby brought to the hospital that same evening has been abandoned. The husband and wife, through the husband's prompting, welcome that child into their lives. As it turns out, the three story lines represent different time periods. The husband and wife are the parents of the twins, and the man looking for his biological father is the now grown baby they took in that night.

It's a moving episode about the power of relationship between spouses, parents and children, siblings, and friends. It ends with a haunting and beautiful song by Sufjan Stevens called "Death with Dignity." The song repeats a simple pattern, incorporating guitar, piano, and a few voices. If you didn't know better, it could be a sad Christmas song, a musical complement to the first Christmas when Mary and Joseph trod silent roads under dark skies. Perhaps they were walking and not talking, wondering where they were going, what it meant to be married, and what their family thought about their getting pregnant before marriage. Or when Jesus was born through suffering in a cold cave where animals bedded down to stay warm, where the only sign of God's presence was the report given to shepherds who had come to see the news. And though we don't know Mary's thoughts, I wonder if, but for a moment, she looked at the starry sky feeling alone that night but also strangely comforted. Perhaps she felt that there were firm, unshakable things in the world with deep, unseen roots. *Your name is Mary. His name is Joseph. And you are held by, and holding, a stronger Savior than either of you can begin to know.*

We were moved by the pain of the episode and the song in particular, the theme that even in death there could be hope. The parents who lost a child but gained a child, the child who lost a father but gained a family, the twins who lost a brother but gained a sibling. Both are true. Both are real. Death and life. Alone and yet not alone. One and yet Three. Two and yet One. A paradox that is held together, not reconciled, but *real.* The guitar and piano go back and forth, back and forth, death and hope, death and hope, like they're hyphenated, *death-hope,* maybe sharing the same substance, maybe producing something new, a new symbol, a new scar—*one flesh.*

Anna and I cried. We pulled out the computer and found the song. Turning out all the lights in our apartment except for the little white lights on our dead Christmas tree, I took her hand in mine. My right arm slid down her side and around her waist, pulling her close. And we danced by the lights on a dead Christmas tree, slowly twirling to the life-death reality that we not only could not ignore but had to embrace.

Anna pulled back, placed both her hands on my face, and looked me in the eyes. She pulled my head gently to the other side. Up until now, her right cheek had rested against my right one. But she switched it so that my scarred left cheek, with bumps and uneven bones, rested on hers. And slowly, she began to move her cheek up and down. Her skin was cool and soft.

At first, as I always did, I felt ashamed. The left side of my face was uneven and did not slide easily against hers. But she kept sliding as we kept twirling. Every now and then she would turn her lips toward me and, just as slowly as we danced, she would kiss my bumps, my jagged bones, and my rough scars, just like that first night so long ago. I would shiver and sink more deeply into that place between her shoulder and face, as if I couldn't hold my body up. We twirled slowly, under the moonlight overlapping the Christmas tree lights and into the darkness. From light into shadow. Both of us tired. Weary. But *there*. Together. As if something new was being born right beneath our feet.

It is not good that we are alone. We look for the *ezer kenegdo* in another, and sometimes we think we find them. But when they fail and the moment moves along, we're simply left with another human, same as us, and a promise to be for them forever. Parents—Children. Wife—Husband. Friend—Friend. Sister—Brother. Jesus—Church.

A song that sounds like death-hope. A child born under starlight, sharing the substance of God himself, a symbol of the promise that God's love is unfailing. A mother and father weary from traveling, cuddling their newborn son to keep him warm. They're all still there in the cold. They're all still there.

There's a word that some theologians have used to describe the Trinity: *perichoresis*. It is the idea of a mutually flowing, surrendering, reciprocating relationship. This idea has even been compared to dancing. God is like a dance.[8] Perhaps as Anna and I danced that evening, God danced with us too. Perhaps for the first time in our marriage, we tapped into the roots of the *ezer kenegdo* and began to discover what it means to be named as one flesh, to reciprocate one another not in our own strength but in Jesus', and in so doing, to see God.

It has nothing to do with the strength or weakness we bring to the partnership. It's simply that we're still fully with one another because God is still fully with each of us first. We say to each other, "I'm still here, my love. I'm not going anywhere. Today, with all my weakness and frailty, I pledge myself to you. With all my selfishness and anger, I lay down my life as best I can. For better or worse, come what may, I refuse to pick my life back up again. Because God laid down his rib in the form of his son. Because Jesus laid down his life for us and has yet to take it back. God pledged himself to us so that I can pledge myself to you."

Perhaps the hyphen is a foxtrot, the rib is a waltz, and a melody the tune of which we're just beginning to learn in the key of brokenness—the tune titled "Love."

Only you, only yours, my Love—forever and always.

Six

The God Who Perfectly Loves Our Imperfections

The first time I met Amberly was at the coffee shop where Anna had just been hired in late fall 2015. Amberly was the shop manager and Anna had come home, bursting with excitement like a kid who made a new friend at school. "Babe, there's this amazing girl at the shop! She's got a gorgeous pixie haircut, perfect smile, and is, like, unbelievably kind." Later, I visited Anna at the coffee shop and verified her report. Amberly's smile was second to none. Her spirit was brimming with kindness. She was a good leader and a selfless soul. As Anna and I got to know her and her boyfriend, Butch, who was as fascinating as she, we learned that Amberly hadn't grown up in a religious family. She had experimented with different religious traditions but left them behind in college. She felt all religion was pointless; it was our job to just treat people with dignity as much as we could.

I still remember the day Anna came home a couple months later, racked with sadness.

"Amberly's leaving the shop," she said. "She's moving on to become a carpenter. A carpenter! How cool is that?"

I, too, was sad. But if a friendship was meant to be, God would cause our paths to cross again, right?

Three things happened in spring 2017, right after Hope Brooklyn's official launch, that were more iterations of God exposing the wounds in my soul and expressing his love within them. The first was a set of stories I read in Luke's Gospel. Hope Brooklyn's numbers had been growing, but just like with my marriage, my identity, and my learning to channel power into powerlessness and trust God's strength, I was exhausted. Anxiety had been coagulating in my chest like lumpy gravy, making it hard to breathe. Whenever a breakthrough happened, it was short-lived.

I don't think I'm alone in this. Have you ever had those moments when you feel like you had an epiphany and rushed home to write it down, only to find your journal and realize you forgot what it was? That was life for me—constantly grabbing my journal and forgetting what happened. It was like stopping the bleeding but not healing the gushing wound that, at the next irritant or facet of my soul, would reopen all over again.

I didn't realize at the time that with every minor breakthrough, God was getting closer to completely healing me. In this season, the continual breaking and gushing of more history was the work of God's grace as his presence and love entered every infected wound of my soul that was keeping me from full communion with him.

The same is true with you. But love is painful because it takes time and energy and our constant "yes" to the Great Surgeon. For me, things began reaching a tipping point around this time, and my anxiety was starting to crack. Ironically, as the church's numbers grew, I became even more fearful. The gravy in me got thicker. That's when I read this triptych of stories in Luke's Gospel.

They revolve around the themes of control and freedom. In each story, a person has multiple things and loses one. To us, no big deal. To the people facing the loss, huge deal. They freak out, inconsolable until they find this lost thing. Whether it's sheep, coins, or a child, they cannot rest until this one lost thing is returned to them (okay, I get the lost child one). They leave everything behind and go in search of the one that was lost. When they find it, their joy is even more intense than their sorrow. The stories demonstrate that you and I are not free—at least not like these people were, which is ironic given the degree of concern they showed over one little lost thing.

When Jesus is with the Pharisees, and the sinners and tax collectors come to listen to him, the Pharisees grumble. They feel superior to others and believe the sinners and tax collectors have wronged them and other Jewish people by selling out to serve Rome and avoid the full demands of God's law. But while they are grumbling, Jesus uses the moment to teach the Pharisees a lesson with one very long, ever-building question:

> Which among you, having one hundred sheep and losing one of them, will not abandon the ninety-nine and go in search for the lost one until you find it? And finding it which of you won't put it around your neck rejoicing? And coming to your house which of you won't call together your friends and neighbors saying to them: "Rejoice with me because I found my lost sheep!" (Luke 15:4-7, author's paraphrase).

While drilling into this story, I thought, *I would never abandon a bigger thing just for the slight chance of finding a smaller thing. Ever. That's the stupidest idea I've ever heard.* Yet even as I made my faux confession, I felt it inside—a release of pressure. Something in Jesus' question startled me to such a degree that it made me laugh.

Has someone ever asked you a question so truthful that it slices through you, and you know they see to your center? You're so caught off guard, nervous and exposed and even a little liberated, that you awkwardly laugh out loud because it feels nice to be really *seen*, even if it's not pretty. You thought you were hiding, but they saw right through you.

You may quietly curse them for being so clairvoyant, but you know they caught you. That's what happened to me. I told Jesus he made no sense, and he gave me a sideways smile like he saw me better than I saw myself. I wanted to both punch him and fall at his feet and cry. Maybe you know what I'm talking about. The question exposed the anxious prison around me and offered me a sight of the blue sky and green grass beyond my bars. In that briefest of moments, I longed to be out there. I wanted to be free so badly. And yet I couldn't let it go.

THE HEARTBREAKING PRISON OF SOCIAL PERFECTIONISM

Most people I know are unhappy. Maybe you're one of them. Keep in mind I'm a pastor. My job is to know people. When I meet with others—older, younger, those firmly in their careers, those just starting off, the rich and the poor—the most common refrain I hear is something along these lines: "I feel like I'm losing in life. Like it's just passing me by. I want to escape from it all." Seriously. So many people feel like they're failing on some level and want out or a do-over. Even those who most would consider "the winners."

In New York I had friends who were executives at tech companies, traders on Wall Street, world class musicians, and actors—the "beautiful people." Sure, sometimes they felt that euphoria of "administrative bureaucracy," as Dostoyevsky called it. They knew they pulled the levers of society, and it gave them a rush when they did. But turn off the spotlights and before long, all they'd talk about was how lonely their life was and how much they felt like a failure. They had wounded souls like the rest of us. We're all searching for the true Mirror to heal our woundedness, and we're all coming up short.

Research backs this up. A survey in June 2019 showed that over the last ten years, in every possible demographic in the West, "deaths of despair" by suicide as well as drug and alcohol abuse have gone up dramatically. We are becoming more self-destructive than ever. This data was before the Covid-19 pandemic, which has only accelerated these trends. The irony is we live in a society that is arguably the freest and plushest history has ever seen—housing, amenities, modern conveniences, the whole nine yards. We have it so good, and yet it seems that the better we have it, the more we hate it and the more our soul is sucked out of us.

Such deaths have skyrocketed most among millennials. The study found that between 2007 and 2017, drug-related deaths in this group increased by 108 percent, alcohol-related deaths by 69 percent, and suicide-related deaths by 35 percent.[1] This doesn't even tell the whole story because there are *twenty times* more attempted suicides than committed suicides. Read that again. For every one person in our country who dies by suicide, there are twenty more who attempt it. This is alarming stuff. On the surface it doesn't make sense. We're finally living in the world our ancestors dreamed about, yet now that we're here, all we want is to get out of it. It's heartbreaking. What's going on?

Will Storr took this question up in his book *Selfie: How We Became So Self-Obsessed and What It's Doing to Us.* He says it's easy to assume anxiety and depression are the culprit for suicide. Today, 8–10 percent of the adult population in the United States or United Kingdom is on antidepressants, which is also a precipitous rise in a short period of time.[2] But an important point is that less than 5 percent of people with depression die by suicide.[3] So mental illness is not exclusively a contributing variable. There are other factors that lead someone to take their life.

Storr interviewed Rory O'Connor, the president of the International Academy of Suicide Research. Over the last twenty years, his team found there is an important variable present in people who die by suicide: social perfectionism.

As O'Connor explains it, "It's not about what you expect of yourself but what *you think others expect of you*." He describes how suicide is as an escape from yourself. The process of wanting to escape begins when the events of your life "fall severely short of standards and expectations."[4] Basically, those who expect little from life find they are constantly surprised with what they get. Those who expect a lot out of their lives never seem to reach what they hoped for. This is perfectionism, a desire to reach some difficult and unreal state of being.

But it's not that people are failing to meet their own expectations. Rather, they are failing to meet what they believe *others* expect of them.

So, where are we getting this idea that others have high expectations of us? I realize some of us come from very demanding families, which makes the answer easy. But I also think for all of us, unfortunately, there's another contributing factor right under our noses. These social expectations are the accumulation of an entire society's worth of narratives curated, airbrushed, algorithmized, and fed to us over the last fifty or more years through our media-saturated lives—through social media, internet, television, or otherwise. They paint a universal and unrealistic picture of what the "good life" should or could be for you and me.

We are more socially isolated from real people than ever before, yet we are more hooked up to technologically constructed, imposturous facades of people than ever before too. As the first sentence in a *New Yorker* article about social media puts it, "Twitter, as everyone knows, is hell."[5] The author writes that the hellish nature of Twitter/X, and all social media, is that everyone on its platform knows none of this is reality and swears to get off, and yet few ever do. Everyone is hooked and secretly hoping, like playing slots at a casino, that their winning number to reach "the perfect life" is just one pull away. But it never comes. And we keep pulling the lever. Or it does come, and we realize that wasn't even what we were looking for. Our lived experience never meets the narratives fed to us of how great our lives could be because, look, here are other people's lives that seem so much better than our own.

It makes sense. You go on some social media site, and what do you see? There's one friend perfectly bronzed, holding a mojito in some paradise destination. You see another sharing those once-in-a-lifetime laughs with their beautiful child while they make sugar cookies. Here's another friend holding up a "Sold" sign because they just bought their first home. And here's one more who, for the heck of it, started exercising today and now has a six-pack! Wow! In the time it took you to see how perfect Shadrach, Meshach, and Abednego are, you sit not tanned in an island paradise but pale in your one-bedroom apartment, not making sugar cookies with your kids because you don't have kids and if you did they would not be that beautiful, not buying a house because you're in debt, and deciding to exchange exercise for this giant tub of peanut butter. Just me?

We're trapped in a prison. And since no one else wants to leave it, we feel like we can't either. I remember a moment early on at Hope Brooklyn that epitomized this for me. I was lamenting having surface-level conversations with people and feeling as if I wasn't making a difference. Usually, I'd return home to Anna after one of these conversations and complain. I'd say I felt like a failure. Then I'd scroll Instagram looking at perfect church pages and try hard not to let my heart churn in my chest with jealousy. This was the "real-time" reality of everyone's church—obviously (cue the sarcasm). But I knew that my subjective experience of planting a church was so different from the images I saw on the 'gram—so much less curated, so much less emotionally appealing, so much duller. In short, I wasn't good enough, which made me unhappy.

It all came to a head one Saturday when I was looking at an image of another church that had baptized someone the previous day. It was a great photo. The waves of the beach were coming over the woman's head, and two men were holding her hands. Her eyes were closed and her face a bit fearful, cheeks blown out preparing for the submersion. The guys were smiling wide. There was a nice filter over the image. And it had generated hundreds of likes and comments of celebration. I should've joined that chorus. I should've beamed at the screen, joyous over what this image meant. I should've fallen to my knees and thanked Jesus that he had revealed himself to another person and she had said *yes*. Instead, I was shocked that this new church, the same age as ours, was already baptizing someone.

I didn't know how to get out of this prison. The magnetic pull toward the perfect life is like trying to swim up a river of molasses or trying to remove yourself from beneath a pile of cement slabs. It's exhausting. We are all addicted to these images of perfection. But why are we obsessed with being the perfect human or church? *No human is perfect!* Then it hit me. I realized that's the point. No *human* is perfect. We're the most socially isolated people who have ever lived because we're isolated from *real* humans. But *machines* are perfect. And we're the most technologically connected society that has ever lived, with technology that is brilliantly coded, inhumanly efficient, and literally impossibly perfect.

Humans aren't efficient; machines are. But also, machines aren't free; humans are. We don't all feel like we're failing at being human. *We all feel like we're failing at being a machine.* We don't want to escape a human existence. We want to escape the machine we're living in. Because that's what our society has built: the logic and the levers, the technologies and the algorithms, the efficiency and the obsession with growth and perfectly marketed, targeted, and synthesized data. We're all being pulled into the mind of a machine. And we're all losing. We've been told that if we keep progressing toward perfection, then we'll be free. But why does no one feel free when we're supposedly the most efficient, most convenient, freest society the world has ever seen? How can that be? The closer we get to society's image of the perfect life, the less free we feel and the more we long to escape it all.

In late fall 2016, Hope Brooklyn had its first preview service. We created a little postcard with a giant stack of pancakes on the front, syrup coming down the side. There were big capital letters boxed in and overlaid on the photo that read, *There's room at the table.* We created a Facebook event, shot it out to anyone and everyone we had met so far, and kept promoting it with blog posts, Instagram posts, and prayer. Then we waited.

The first preview service came and went, and it was precisely what you'd expect from people who had never started a church. We had forgotten to register our PowerPoint technology. We filled perhaps 25 percent of the auditorium. The band was a little off-key. We talked about the prodigal son, who was lost and came home to an incredible reception from his father and his village. My sermon was a little long. Okay, it was a lot long. Then we had Communion and ate pancakes, blowing a bunch of fuses in the process. It was a very imperfect day, and it would have been easy to get discouraged. However, in the midst of such imperfection, I looked at the congregation—and sitting in the second row in the middle of the auditorium were Amberly and Butch. We were stunned with gladness.

THE FREEDOM IN INEFFICIENCIES

The second thing that happened that spring of 2017 was a conversation I had with my brother Matthew, who, when younger, had run as fast and as far from God as possible— the prodigal son. In high school and college, he was reckless, cruel, selfish, and self-destructive. This behavior played out until he was twenty-seven when an old friend saw him at rock bottom and invited him to his church's small group. Matt went. Six months later, he experienced the love of God in his wounded soul and began to follow Jesus.

Matt told me about being at our grandmother's church when a homeless man entered by the side door and promptly took off his dirty, well-worn shoes. The organ played and the congregation sang a hymn. Matt couldn't stop looking at the man. The congregants confessed, were absolved, and passed the peace. Matt watched the man.

When it came time for the pastor to deliver the sermon, the man slipped out of his pew, headed toward the door, put on his shoes, and exited quietly.

"I was amazed," said Matt, weeping on the phone as he processed what he'd seen. "I don't take off my shoes, Russ. He did."

I tried to rationalize Matt's keeping on his shoes.

"You're showing up with Grandma," I said. "The man's shoes were dirty. There could be any number of reasons. You didn't do anything wrong."

"But he understood where he was entering, Russ. He took off his shoes. And I never take off mine."

Then I realized he didn't need me rationalizing his behavior. My brother needed to repent. God was reminding Matthew that not too long ago, he had been that man welcomed into God's holy presence with dirty shoes. Not too long ago, Matt would've taken his shoes off without a second thought at the dawning realization of how much God loved him even in the life he had lived.

As he cried and spoke, I was breaking inside too. I was catching another glimpse beyond my own prison cell, because I'd realized an uncomfortable truth: it had been a long time since I'd removed my spiritual shoes in the house of God too. Why? Because that's just not what you do if you're chasing social perfection. That's not what others expect.

When did we all start living inside the mind of a machine, believing that freedom is found in us becoming perfect?

Theologian Jacques Ellul took up this question in many of his books, most notably in *The Technological Society*. In it, he puts forth an idea called "technique," which is the belief that there is one right way to do something. Essentially, we should all think, act, and behave like machines. We should eliminate inefficiencies; we should squeeze every drop out of a thing, a business, our very lives. It is as J. R. R. Tolkien put it in one of his letters: "The most widespread assumption of our time: if a thing can be done, it must be done."[6] If there is room for something to be maximized—money, time, an idea—it *must be maximized*. To not maximize something would be a waste of potential, and anything wasted, even potential, is a sin. And yes, note the irony that there is plenty of other "waste" created in our obsession with continual maximized efficiency.

Why would we want this type of world? I think it's obvious. The logic of a machine is all about *control*. Control is about making everything predictable and eliminating surprises. Our society is now premised on the belief that *we are most free when we are most in control*. To be in control of your life in every facet—your family, your career, your body, and everyone's perception of your life too—is to be constrained by no one, to be determined by no one. It is to be free. But it's not working.

When you say, "I feel like I'm losing," you're really saying, "I'm trying to be perfectly in control of how people see me, but I can't hold it together. My marriage is not perfect. My kids are not perfect. My career trajectory is not perfect. My faith is not perfect. My body is not perfect. I'm wounded. There are so many inefficiencies and imperfections in all these places. And I'm working as hard as I can to hold it all together, but I'm going to be found out and exposed. Someone's going to ask me a question and it'll be revealed they see right through me. They'll slice off my façade. It's going to crack and crumble into dust. They'll see my wounds and then they'll reject me. I can't keep this up much more. The more control I seek to exert over my personal maximization or how people perceive me, the less free I feel."

Do you see the paradox? The more you try to be in control, the more you're the one being controlled.

The third thing that happened was that Amberly and Butch kept showing up. It was encouraging and confusing at the same time. One Sunday after service, Amberly came up to me in tears and fell into my arms. She wept for thirty seconds, pulled back, and walked away without saying a thing. She started asking for book or podcast recommendations and would say things like, "I can see why the sacrifice of Jesus is such a profound display of love, but I can't get over the creation story or sexism in the Bible."

The four of us started meeting together. Anna and I never tried to convince Amberly of anything. We just shared why Jesus' love was so compelling for us as he met us in our wounds and imperfections. Amberly kept stirring and asking questions. Most of all, she kept showing up. Almost every Sunday, she and Butch would be there in the second row in the middle of the auditorium. She usually didn't sing. But I could always tell she was listening. She was taking it in, and something was moving inside her too.

That spring and summer of 2017, we did a sermon series called "Questions." The congregation anonymously texted their most pressing questions about God, the Bible, Jesus, faith, whatever. It was based on my belief that if God is truly who he says he is and is as strong as he says he is, we don't need to be afraid of hard questions.

We don't need to be afraid of challenging topics. God can handle the full weight of our doubt and confusion. He can defend himself; we don't need to control his public image. The beautiful irony of the series and that time was that it was all about setting the gospel free and not controlling God or forcing him into some prison of our own making. What's more, God was slowly setting me free too. I was anxious and afraid, and he was revealing how I was still held captive by the logic of the perfect machine that I could not realize in my life. I was just too imperfect of a person.

One day, a particularly hard day for me, Amberly texted Anna and me. She said, "I'm halfway through your last sermon and loving it. I feel like this series has really resonated and been super strong for me. Still struggling with a lot of this whole 'Christianity' thing, but thank you both for creating a community that gives space and encourages questions. I love you both so much and am so happy you're in my life."

It was salve to my wounds, another moment of relief. Because I felt as if I was failing as a pastor, as if Hope Brooklyn was not a perfect church, and no matter how hard I tried I could not eliminate our imperfections, my imperfections.

But here was another sight of the green grass and blue sky just outside the socially perfect expectations that barred my heart from truly being free.

THE PERFECT LOVE FOUND IN INEFFICIENT DECISIONS

Let's go back to Luke's story about the sheep. Jesus is talking to the Pharisees and scribes while sinners and tax collectors are coming to him. The Pharisees are more like the machine, concerned with controlling the religious game, producing an efficient society of religiously perfect Jewish people, and keeping score so they know who is winning—them, of course.

The Pharisees and scribes are concerned with establishing and maintaining their expectations of perfection within a system of clean-shoed moralists. But the sinners and tax collectors have opted out of the game. They are tired of being controlled and always feeling like they can't measure up to the winners of society, and so they live according to different standards and measures. In a way, they are a little freer than the Pharisees, but not completely. Not yet. So as the sinners and tax collectors come to Jesus, the Pharisees and scribes grumble. To which Jesus poses his antagonizing, liberating question.

It's astonishing on multiple levels. First, the Pharisees imagine that the sinners have wronged them by sidling up to Rome and removing themselves from the community of faithful, Torah-observing Jews. But Jesus' image is of a shepherd desperate for every single sheep to be safe home in the flock. No heart of bitterness or offense there! Then, Jesus talks about the shepherd noticing that one sheep out of one hundred was missing. At the time of my reading, Hope Brooklyn's numbers were around the same, and I felt like I couldn't notice everyone. In the biblical story, how did this shepherd notice that *one sheep* was missing when he had so many?

Finally, Jesus says the shepherd *forsakes* the ninety-nine to go in search of that lost one. He doesn't leave the one behind; he forsakes the others. It's not a question in the shepherd's mind that he's got to go after the one sheep. His heart doesn't even consider an alternative. Which is incredible because I felt we had worked hard to gather a flock of one hundred people, and what Jesus was asking me wasn't a question at all. It was a statement.

This image Jesus uses of a grieving shepherd desperately going after his lost sheep no matter the risk or cost is in stark contrast to the Pharisees, who are committed to maintaining control over the moral lives of Israel and are angry at those who have defected. It's almost as if they are so committed to keeping order and control that they aren't free to simply love the sheep.

Here's how I imagined Jesus talking to me in that season: *Hey, Russell. Hope Brooklyn has about one hundred people. One hundred beautiful people. But there are many more who have run from me. I'm concerned you're so focused on keeping this thing together that you're forgetting the heart of the shepherd, who would do anything for the one. So stop trying to control it and let it all go, if only one person could be found by me, seen by me, loved by me, and brought back into my love. If you viewed Hope Brooklyn not as a machine to be controlled but as people to dearly love an inordinate and inefficient amount, the joy that would fill every heart would be deep, real, and liberating! You'd feel like a free human being. Right now, you don't. You feel paranoid and anxious because you're holding together the threads of some unrealistic image of perfection. In your heart, go after the one and I promise you'll be free and alive. Why? Because you'll no longer be motivated by control but by love. The Good Shepherd seeks not to control his flock but to love every one of his sheep.*

The fear that grips your heart and says you cannot make a mistake is a stultifying prison. If you want to be completely free, then do something imperfect, something the machines can't predict or systematize or create algorithms for. Do something that makes no sense to the efficient mind. Don't control the game like the Pharisees. Abandon the ninety-nine like the shepherd; go after the one. Take off your shoes; leave before the sermon. Don't grow a church because you think you control a machine; let God be in control while you're busy loving him and his people. That, my friends, is perfect freedom. And that is precisely what God did for us.

God's love in Jesus did not grow his following but shrank it—not intentionally, of course. Jesus was just too busy obeying and loving his Father. His disciples left him. His people rejected him. The world turned its face against him. Even God seemingly abandoned him. The "likes" dried up. The subscribers stopped watching. Yet at every step, Jesus continued to lay down control—control of his image, control of the narrative, control of the world, and control of his life for the sake of love.

Love does not control; Love gives up control for the beloved. Love doesn't see a flock; Love sees every sheep. Love doesn't see a mass; Love sees people to heal, people to teach, people to kiss, friends with whom to share life. Love takes off its shoes every time, in every place, everywhere. Love is willing to lose it all going after one sheep because it doesn't see *all*; it simply sees *one*. In fact, says Jesus, *Love did lose it all going after one sheep.* For even in a heaven full of ninety-nine faithful, loyal creatures, even with the power that could destroy and create all over again, God noticed one sheep, this small speck of his creation, had wandered off, and he couldn't live while that was the case. So Jesus left the flock and came after us.

Freedom is not found by becoming perfectly in control; freedom is found when you receive Jesus' perfect love in your imperfect life. When you receive God's perfect love, you don't have to play the game anymore. You've already won. You don't have to fight so hard to be perfect or viewed as perfect by others to fill your wounded soul. Rather, your soul is healed because you're perfectly loved. You can enjoy life with the Shepherd now. Nothing is required of you to be loved, though everything will be asked of you to live in that love. Through love and by love, you can grow into the image of God's perfect love.

There's a lot packed into that. But no need to fret or stress about learning all that is entailed yet. He'll reveal it in time. Right now, just remove your shoes and take a walk in the grass, for Christ has set you free. Go, you imperfect human—go and be free with Jesus.

FRIENDS WHO FREELY DANCE—WITHOUT SHOES

If our wounded soul creates a desire to be perfectly in control, and the kiss is when we realize God has already set us free in our imperfections through his perfect love, then the scar is how that friendship begins to transform us into the image of perfect love. What do free, shoeless, loving friends do? They dance!

In the parable after the shepherd finds the lost sheep, Jesus says, "Then he calls his friends and neighbors together and says, 'Rejoice with me; I have found my lost sheep.' I tell you that in the same way there will be more rejoicing in heaven over one sinner who repents than over ninety-nine righteous persons who do not need to repent" (Luke 15:6-7).

In short, free people celebrate. The game has been won. It's over. We are loved by the Shepherd who came and paid our ransom to bring us back home. That love has set us free. Let us rejoice! We do not need to strive anymore. We can now enjoy the walk back toward the heavenly flock, basking in his love.

According to historian Barbara Ehrenreich, Christians of the first and second centuries "met in people's homes, where their central ritual was a shared meal that was no doubt washed down by Jesus' favorite beverage, wine. There is reason to think that they sang too . . . [and] very likely, Christians also danced."[7] The first Christians were known by the ritualized nature of their gatherings, which involved feasting, singing, and dancing.

Does that sound like a people trying to control how they're perceived or a people who already know they are perfectly loved? In a class of his I took, Tim Keller explained once that he was indebted to professor Bert Hornback, who pointed out that the words *free* and *friend* are etymologically related. That is, Keller said, "we set our friends free by our love for them." Love, which is willing to give up control for its friends, is the expression of true, inward freedom. This is precisely what God did for us: he gave up control to set us free. Now, he asks us to give up our control to enter this freedom—to celebrate, sing, feast, and dance as a sign of our love. To celebrate in a world still longing for perfection is to give up control of our lives and their outcomes. I'm not talking about partying, which is perverted celebration. It's the despairing inverse of a soul that knows it will never be perfect, and so it says, "What the heck, let's live for today." Partying is escapism. But celebration is a sign of true freedom because it is the fruit of a soul that has accepted God's love in its imperfections. Celebration is the fullness of joy.

We started dancing at Hope Brooklyn. The school we met in wasn't a glamorous space, but we brought the funk. We hung streamers and balloons, put up a photo booth, hired a DJ, set out a spread, and danced during our brunch times after service. We would dance for our anniversaries, end-of-year galas, Easter, and Christmas. Any excuse for a dance party, we came up with one.

One time, our staff choreographed a flash mob–style dance to kick off the party. I'm telling you, friends, you have not tasted freedom until you've danced sober in an elementary school cafeteria at noon on a Sunday. Pure liberation. We danced and ate and celebrated because God was for us and we were living into the assurance of his friendship that could not be taken away, no matter how imperfect our lives.

To be clear, dancing didn't cure my social perfectionism. (Though if you saw my dance moves, you might wonder what else would!) I still struggled with controlling Hope Brooklyn like a machine. I still measured myself by the logic of efficiency and growth. I cared what people thought of me. So, Anna and I instituted something else that attempted to cultivate an eye for the one instead of the ninety-nine. Every

Sunday after church, we named three things to celebrate. Usually, they were little signs that God was at work in our community: This person showed up after a while away. That person brought a friend. The band really worshiped in this song. The brunch was delicious. After naming these things, we prayed for individual people.

The crazy thing is that the more we were looking for it, the more we saw it. We saw God move. We saw love so active in our community that it made us laugh. We saw one person return to church after many years away. We saw them come forward to pray with the prayer team. We saw a couple stay for brunch and laugh together when they had not laughed much as of late. We saw questions emerge from the lips of those who grew up atheist or agnostic. We saw tears in the eyes of those angry with God and the slightest movement in their hands as they loosened their fingers into the posture of an open palm. We saw eyes shut and words flow as lips whispered lyrics of songs they hadn't sung in so long—or ever.

The more I saw these little things, the freer I felt and the harder I prayed to see and count as Jesus does. I prayed to see the one even as I pastored many. I prayed to be filled with more unpredictable, inefficient love for people that they would meet Jesus, enter his loving lordship, and find freedom in their identity as his perfectly beloved ones. As my eyes shifted to the smaller and inefficient things, the church grew. Or at least I think it did. I can't be sure because whether it did or not, it grew in my heart. I felt freer.

One day, we decided to take our prayers to the next level. We had been forming a community for almost a year, and though there were many people who didn't identify as Christian—which was a good sign because it showed we were loving them well and asking the right questions—none of them had become followers of Jesus, either. We felt led by God to pray strongly for one person in our community who had never received Jesus to yield to his loving lordship, to give up control of their lives, and to let themselves be found by him. We didn't pray for anyone specifically—just that one person would be found by Jesus. I remember it clearly because the very next Sunday after we prayed that prayer, it happened.

The sermon ended, and I invited people up for Communion. Every Sunday we took Communion together, saying the table is a symbol of a heart's confession that Jesus is Lord—*Jesus' love is perfectly in control*—and is open to all free of cost. As the song played, I began to distribute.

The body of Christ broken for you. The blood of Christ shed for you. The body for you. The blood for you.

Out of nowhere, I looked up and there was Amberly in line. Whenever we took Communion at the end of service, she always stayed respectfully in her seat. But today, for the first time ever, she came forward. She had a slight smile on her face and tears in her eyes. I lost my voice and my throat caught for a second. *The body of Christ broken for you.* She took the bread. *The blood of Christ shed for you.* She dipped the bread and ate it without another look back.

Later that day, Anna and I were stunned about what had happened. *What are the odds?* we wondered. Not even one Sunday had passed from when we had started praying specifically for someone to meet Jesus and this would be the Sunday she finally gave her life to him. I decided to text her.

"You don't have to say anything if you're not ready. But you came forward for Communion, and you never do. What's up?"

She replied, "I got tired of saying no."

And as I looked out my prison window, I saw Jesus emerge over the grassy knoll with a sheep around his shoulders, laughing and crying and dancing in his dirty frock—shoeless. I could barely make out his voice in the distance.

"I found her!" He laughed and did a little whirl, tapping his toes. "I found her!"

The bars were gone. The wind was cool and perfect, so I prepared to go out and meet them. But as I stepped outside, before going a step further, I sat down on the grass and slowly began to untie my shoes.

Seven

The God Who Went First

When I was seventeen, I asked a girl out from my youth group for the third and—I told myself—final time. We were going on our church's winter youth retreat where she and I were both leaders. The previous few months we had been together in preparation for it, so we had built a fun friendship. And most importantly of all, I had completed "the big one."

For Goldenhar syndrome patients, "the big one" is the colloquial term for the major operation they will need to undergo at some point in their lives. Growing up with an underdeveloped face, I had experienced numerous surgeries to restore utility to my jaw, cheeks, and ears. But when children undergo these operations, they still have a lot of growing to do. Consequently, the Goldenhar patient's face becomes distorted. In my case, I developed a wicked crossbite because my rib bone—which had become my left jaw at age eight—grew twice as fast and twice as large. My face elongated, leaving callow pockmarks and exposing the lack of fat in my left cheek. A protruding bone by my left ear grew larger, giving the appearance of a tumor.

When I elected to undergo "the big one" at sixteen, I had high hopes. The surgery went as planned. Afterward, however, it was a long healing process. Pain seeped into my everyday life, though I assumed that was simply the price I'd have to pay for a "better face." But as the swelling subsided with each passing day, so did my hope. Healing, I was learning, wasn't one of those things where you wake up one morning and you're pleasantly surprised by what you see. It was a slow process. Two months after the surgery, it dawned on me that I wasn't going to wind up with the face I'd hoped for. It was still going to look very different from other people's. I was pleased with the progress but let down, too, because the improvement wasn't as vast as I'd hoped.

In many ways, youth group was my safe place. I was a leader there and I genuinely encountered the presence of God, which never seemed contingent on feelings about my face. It was a wonderful space full of God's love and good friendships. And of course, as a seventeen-year-old kid, I had plenty of crushes.

What I wanted most of all was this girl to go out with me. I decided I was going to ask her to my prom. I had asked her out before and she had kindly said no. But that was before "the big one," I reasoned. This time, after all I had endured to get the right face, my prayer and hope was that she would say yes.

I underwent one more surgery that winter before the re-treat to inject fat into my left cheek to create as symmetrical a face as possible. When the winter retreat arrived, I kept trying to get her alone and ask her. I think she sensed as much because whenever we were alone, she'd find a reason to leave. She was sweet and never rude. But I could tell she suspected what I was up to and was trying to protect herself—and, perhaps, me.

The retreat concluded, and I had one last chance before we went our separate ways. A group of us had left our cars at my house. We hung out for a bit, reminiscing and laughing about the weekend until everyone slowly dispersed, leaving the two of us alone. My now-or-never moment had arrived. *Ask now, ask now.* But I couldn't. I was too afraid. I didn't want to be rejected again.

She looked away and mumbled something about having to go. As she drove off, I cursed myself and walked upstairs to my room. The prospect of texting her, though not as ro-mantic, emerged as a safer option. I'd play it cool. *Oh, hey, I meant to talk to you about this, but I totally forgot to ask! Are you interested in going to prom with me? Should be a good time.* Something like that.

I typed the message, took a breath, and hit send. I threw my phone on my bed and forced myself to walk down-stairs to get a glass of water. I needed to wait five minutes. I couldn't do it. After perhaps two, I sprinted back upstairs and grabbed my phone. She had texted back. In those first few nanoseconds, I was pumped. Maybe I'd overthought this whole thing. Then I looked at her response.

Hey! Haha. That's super sweet. Unfortunately, I'm already busy that weekend! I'm sorry.

My heart dropped like a broken elevator. I read her text at least ten times, seeing if there was any way to salvage this. There wasn't. She was clear. I felt the tears coming, so I closed my door and sat on the floor against my bed. She really may have been busy. I'll never know. But on that night, all I felt and heard was, *Russell, you're sweet. But you're ugly and I can't go out with an ugly guy.*

Do you know this kind of pain? On some level, I imagine you do. We all do. The previous months of pain and recovery, progress and growth, and stupid, foolish hope poured out of me like mud on a hillside. I lay down on the floor and cried for a long, long time. I also prayed. My prayers and my tears intersected. Something along the lines of, *God, do you love me?* I didn't feel a yes, but I didn't feel a no, either. I just felt like there was more to the story than he was letting on, and it was okay that I felt very sad. He also felt very sad. So I just lay there.

AN INVITATION TO GO DEEPER
INTO THE HEART OF THINGS

Fall 2017, after Hope Brooklyn launched, Anna and I were gassed. We had burned both ends of the candle and our hands were singed. God had been shattering us, more me than her, and though some powerful breakthroughs had occurred, there was still much discovery and pain to process.

Our marriage wasn't horrible, but it wasn't great, and we knew we needed someone to listen and help us see what we could not. So we began to see a Christian counselor. She was an older woman from Queens named Lindy with a broad smile and long, thin hair. She spoke softly in a metronome cadence that made me never feel judged. One of the first times we were there, she looked at me tranquilly and said, "Russell, it seems that you have tremendous amounts of anxiety and anger." She said it like an invitation for me to acknowledge what I'd always known.

I don't think you've processed your face fully. Why don't we spend some time doing that?

So for the next few weeks I went back in time, exploring stories like the one I just shared that had to do with deep, painful wounds in my soul stemming from the brokenness found in my Goldenhar syndrome.

When I was eight, I told her, I had a friend named Joseph who had huge mood swings. At times, he was a great friend; at other times, he was cruel and teased me mercilessly. He would walk behind me at recess, laughing and pointing. When I turned around and told him to stop, he'd grab his left hand and yank back at his left cheek, pulling it taut to make it look disfigured like my own. He'd point at me and laugh.

"Joseph, stop it!" I'd say. "Why are you doing this?"

He'd just laugh. He was too far gone in those moments. Later, I'd come to realize that he was lost in his own instability and pain, his own woundedness, to come out of it. Hurt people hurt people, the preachers say. Don't we ever. I told myself that it wasn't me, it was him. But I didn't believe it. Because, truly, it *was* me. My face *did* look like that.

It's been said that mythology is at the heart of things.[1] For us, myth means fiction, detached from reality. But in the ancient Greek sense, a myth—from the word *mythos*—is "the story that announces the true state of things, what is factual, what really happened."[2] Myths are how we make sense of our worlds beyond the data we can gather.

> History is the story of events that played out in civilization, but myths are expressions of the human heart. The themes and archetypes of our myths transcend time and culture. They arise from unconscious instincts . . . and they therefore teach us about what it means to be human on the deepest level.[3]

Our lives are full of personal, familial, and societal myths that offer explanations for why things are the way they are. The Israelis and Palestinians can't get along because of the ancient myth surrounding Abraham's children and the true inheritors of the land. There's so much more to the story than that, but this simple narrative somehow speaks to an even deeper part of our souls than the data can reach.

Perhaps you believe that your family has been broken and emotionally avoidant for generations because of a great-grandfather who was an abusive alcoholic. Of course, there is much more to the generational tale. But something about that narrative and the subsequent plotlines that have poured out of it seems *right*.

My personal myth was that people did not love me because of my ugly face. While it was true people struggled to see beyond my face, it was also true that many people were wonderfully close to me. Yet I naturally gravitated to the "they don't love me" side of the ledger. Even though the myth put far too tidy of a bow on a far more complex situation, that's the narrative that *stuck*. Our myths arise from the deep, unconscious instincts of the human soul beyond what our limited minds and data collection can process. Myths are the deep, spiritual hungering that emerge from human hearts that help us make sense of our lives, families, and worlds.

What are your myths? Go deeper. Do you believe people are untrustworthy because your father walked out on your family? Do you believe you are second best as a human because the world seems to prefer your sister? Do you believe you're dumb because your teacher laughed when you asked that one question, humiliating you in front of the class? Do you believe you're fundamentally broken because of that addiction you still cannot leave behind? Do you believe you're a failure because your parents never said they were proud of you? Do you believe you're damnable because of that decision you made that destroyed another's life?

We all have myths—narratives that explain *who* we are, *why* we are, and *how* we are. Whether they're true or partly true, they are powerful and shape our entire lives, and they often are the source of our deepest wounds.

Here's why it's important you name your myth: if God is going to truly reveal himself to you in a way that will set you free and change your life, you will have to find him smack dab in the middle of it. I've found many of the other lesser myths are gathered up in a major one, and until you find God's love in that one, you won't be fully healed.

But don't worry—he's already there.

THE MYTH THAT PUT ON FLESH

The details surrounding Jesus' life aren't unique. The trope of a demigod who lives, performs miracles, teaches, dies, and resurrects is actually a common one found in myths around the ancient world. I don't say this to scare you. Again, myth does not mean fiction. It means truth beyond what our conscious minds can grasp. The dying and rising Savior is not unique as a story. And since all of us come from one God, I would expect as much.

But the account of Jesus Christ is unique in one regard—it *really happened*. Jesus of Nazareth was a historical person who lived in historical Galilee, died under a historical proconsul named Pontius Pilate, and was raised from a historical tomb outside Jerusalem. What is unique about Jesus is not that the details around his story are *mythic* but that they are also *history*. The Myth-became-flesh.

This matters because in Jesus' story we see all our deepest hungers reflected right back at us. We see what we wished our lives looked like had we known a perfect Mirror. In Jesus, we see a human whose inner world was filled with God, not blocked and clogged with wounds. In Jesus, we see what we wish was our personal myth—that he was the beloved child of God, fully known and chosen. This meant he was fully free to love others with the power of God's presence, which was stronger than the forces of darkness that wounded God's world—and us.

He could heal diseases, cast out demons, teach in ways that opened minds, act in ways that angered the darkness in the world, touch our core wounds, and upset social and political norms that kept people separated and oppressed. He lived a life that only the one true God could have lived because it was totally free of brokenness, sin, and the wounds that emerge as a result. It was a life in perfect relationship with God. It was the perfect Myth—the true story of all things.

But as we said in the beginning, we also see Jesus end his perfect life imperfectly. We see Christ die a gruesome death on a cross. In all four Gospels, we hear him say over and over that his life's purpose was not the healings, nor the teachings, nor whatever his disciples imagined it to be. His life's purpose was toward one end—*death*. And in the crucifixion, we reach the epicenter of it all.

The wounds I've recounted in this book were the various myths through which I viewed the world and myself. They were the interpretive framework by which I found my purpose in the universe. Wounded myths like finding my identity in others' validation of me, feeling shame in being an outside church planter, grappling with how to build a church family bigger than our respective culture, or relentlessly pursuing perfection in a machine instead of love between humans. All these wounded myths were the narratives I believed about the world, myself, and God. And here's the interesting thing I was learning: God had a role in these myths. But he was more like a bit character. He had loved me in some of my wounds, but he hadn't yet met me in *the Wound*—the place where all the wounded myths came from.

There was a reason I believed my validation came from what I achieved. There was a reason I sought out perfection and misused my power. There was a central wound that gave rise to all these other wounds. God had accomplished small victories, but they were just that—smaller battles amid a greater war. He was marching forward, preparing to meet me in the deepest part of my soul and deliver his verdict there.

Which means he had to meet me at the cross—my cross. The crucifixion story is the epicenter from which all the other wounds emerge. The crucifixion is the place where God and humanity were separated from one another—life from death. But it's also where God enters all of humanity's wounded souls at their deepest level. It's the place of the separation and the restoration. And for those with ears to hear, the crucifixion story is where God enters *your* soul, once and for all.

THE TRUTH AT THE CENTER OF THE WOUND

I continued to see Lindy through the fall. We met in a clean, white-tiled building in Hell's Kitchen, an avenue west of the turbulence of Times Square. The building was owned by a Christian couple whose heart was for it to be a place of refuge and healing at the epicenter of a hard city. They called it *Coram Deo*—in the presence of God.

My counselor and I explored my memories, specifically those regarding my face. Interestingly, though I spoke confidently about my face to others, I was appalled at how inarticulate I was when it came to exploring my emotions around it. I had never allowed myself to feel anything about my face. Instead, I would immediately spin the narrative, talk about how I overcame the setbacks, and declare how my trials had made me stronger, what I had learned from my operations, and so on. But I had never just *felt* anything about it. As we circled closer to those possible feelings, I grew increasingly agitated. I felt unstable. I had a sneaking suspicion that I wasn't going to like what I found or what I felt there. If I removed the dam in my soul where the emotions over my broken face were, I would be engulfed with forces beyond my control. I would drown in the revelation. But I had no choice.

"What's your earliest memory of the hospital?" Lindy asked. I looked outside at a gray tree trunk surrounded by stone pebbles. It was an overcast day, milk white and sad.

"When I was six years old, I had my first of three ear reconstruction surgeries in San Francisco," I told her. "I had already had other operations up to that point—tonsils and adenoids, skin tags, sewing up my mouth, that sort of stuff. But this was the first one I remember possessing a different gravitas. Grandma and Papa had driven down from Lexington to keep my brothers while Mom, Dad, and I were in California. I was excited to go to San Francisco. We were flying on an airplane that had TV screens. Dad said we could see a Giants game. We'd head down to the boardwalk and feed the seals, eat seafood, and visit the aquarium. We were staying with friends who worked for the YMCA like my dad. They had two sons who had Super Nintendo.

"I was excited for the trip. But it wasn't a vacation because, of course, I had to have a surgery. Doctors were going to cut open my stomach and remove a rib. They were going to take skin from my butt and lay it over that rib that had been formed into an ear like papier-mâché. It was going to be painful, they said. I wouldn't be able to play basketball for a while. I didn't think about these things. The aquarium and Super Nintendo were far too exhilarating to think about. The pain would be fast; that's what I told myself. I would take a deep breath and get back to Super Mario as quickly as I could."

She nodded. "Go on." I didn't want to, but I did.

"The day of the surgery came. I was sitting in the bed, waiting to be wheeled back to the operating room. Mom was perched in a chair by the window, reading a book. Dad and I were playing dots. The TV was on, and cartoon laughter filled the room. Nurses and doctors came and went, always doing the same thing, checking clipboards, asking how I was feeling, touching my toes, smiling—always smiling."

"What do you feel right now?" Lindy asked. "The boy in the bed—what does he feel?"

Something moved inside me. A quick contortion. A shot of discomfort. I hadn't thought about what the boy felt—what I felt. There was nothing to *feel*. There was only something to *do*: get through it. What was he feeling? What was I feeling?

"I don't know what I'm feeling," I said.

I took a deep breath, steadying my uncomfortable emotions, trying to be inside my body, to enter my myth. I thought of a recurring dream I had been having all fall in which I was trying to escape a dark sense of resignation and apathy.

"Close your eyes," she said.

I did, and I was there again. I was back in the hospital room, standing off in a corner watching the six-year-old me sit in his bed and await the pain to come. In the counselor's room, I began to cry.

"What are you feeling?" she asked.

"I feel anger. A lot of anger. Everyone is lying. No one is telling the truth."

In the hospital room, a nurse comes in with a small vial of purple liquid. "It tastes like grape juice," she says to the boy. She's lying. The boy drinks it and immediately grimaces. It actually tastes like bitter chalk.

He begins to chew his sheets to get rid of the taste as his dad strokes his hair. I look around the room, and all I see is deception. Contorted faces beneath sympathetic smiles, like the grins of the demonic masked by faked faces of empathy. I see the IV in the little boy's hand.

"That's the worst part—the IV. It signals that he is no longer in control. He's not human anymore. He's now . . . what is he? He's subhuman. He can't keep himself alive. The sticky tape that won't go anywhere. The needle just sitting in his hand puncturing his skin as if it's a friend. Worst friend ever. Just like Joseph, my so-called friend who mocked my face in front of classmates. As if it's normal. To this day I don't wear jewelry. Never could. I hate things hindering me. Things that are encumbrances to my body."

In the vision, I look at the boy who is sitting there watching everything and understanding nothing. But something is different; something is birthing inside him, and he knows it. He just doesn't know what. I watch the boy with angry tears in my eyes, knowing that as soon as he falls asleep, or is put to sleep, rather, he will awaken in terrible pain and his body will be covered with sticky stuff. Electrodes, clamps on his fingers, beeping sounds, tape and gauze, pain, so much pain. I don't feel sorry for the boy. I feel indifference toward him.

He'll be fine. He is tougher than anyone realizes. But to the rest, I feel anger. I want to fight. The IV—that dreadful IV— was the start of all of it. It was the first tear in his inner world. It was as if they bound him and led him away.

I look at my parents. The rage falls like a sheet of water, and I am filled with sadness and longing. My mother, sitting there with helpless eyes. I have never seen the helplessness until now. She is pretending to read her book. But I can see it now—she's terrified. *Mama*, I whisper in the vision. They are the words of one who understands now that he can't protect her from the pain she's facing, either. All he wants is to climb up into her arms and bury his head in her chest, to escape from it all and fall asleep. There is a piercing in her soul too, and no one can protect her. It is her burden to bear as the boy's mother.

There's Dad. The man with the short black hair and tight jawline who had no father growing up and resolved, by God, he would look after and protect his sons. Naturally, he's sitting as close to his son as possible—yet he's really worlds away from him. Like a man who follows his master into a courtyard only to discover the rooster's call is enough to break his strength, he cannot protect the boy no matter how much his rage tells him he can. He cannot save him no matter how much he will fight to do so. The man desperately in search of righteousness, love, and justification is utterly separated from all three. He would die for his son. Yet he has no power to stop what is about to happen.

The boy's parents are smiling at him, holding his hand, laughing with him, but now I can see the truth. They are so terribly afraid, so powerless and weak. How had I not seen it before? The fear is literally quivering out of their eyes.

The nurses are in their cartoon-printed scrubs with big grins and clipboards. They are tired. They have more surgeries to perform, an endless barrage of patients who will suffer right in front of them, patients who they will save and don't deserve it, patients who they must guard their souls against or their souls will be crushed. They smile as best as they can. But on some level, the boy has to be a tally on a ledger that allows them to maintain emotional control. I wonder if they are unable to explore the depths of what is before them. They simply have to keep order and do the best they can to protect their own positions and find the courage to show up day after day.

In just a few minutes, they will wheel this boy back into an all-white room. It will be without couches, books, and Super Nintendo. The light will be sharp. The furniture will be cold and hard. It will be full of people walking around preparing trays of instruments for torture—short bludgeoning ones, tall sharp ones, scissors with hooked noses. There will be tall light-post contraptions full of beeping sounds filling the room. And everyone will be there for one reason: the cutting open of this boy.

They'll laugh and tell jokes and he'll try and be comfortable, but he'll be very cold without clothes, holding his Mickey Mouse doll tightly. Many hands will grab him and lift him up from his warm bed. They'll splay him out on the cold, metallic table and then raise it into the air, the sound of a slow lifting. Those many hands will do whatever they want to his body—touching him, arranging his legs, uncrossing his arms—as the table slowly buzzes closer to that singular, all-seeing eye of light. And all will gaze upon him.

They'll mark his body with ink and speak softly to him about basketball. They'll say things in another language— medical things about heart rates and tools and procedures. The smells, oh, the smells: horrible scents of iodine and alcohol, of sanitation and false health, like sour wine on a sponge of hyssop. They'll bring a mask to his face, and there will be many hands holding him down. "Breathe slowly," they'll say. "Count backward." The air he'll breathe is sweet. It'll tickle his throat. And as he counts and breathes that evil air, fear filling his lungs with every breath because there's nothing he can do to fight back, he'll gaze upon at least six heads moving all around him in every direction. Their forms will slowly merge into that bright and terrible light, which will grow brighter and brighter until the entire room is plunged into darkness.

Holding his Mickey tightly, right before he loses consciousness, he'll see a flash of brown hair, the quick blur of color in her sweater. Her head will swing around, and she'll gaze at him with a look of terrified relief. She'll fall onto her knees and reach out her long arms and soft hands as wide as they will go, begging him to come to her. In that moment, with the light filling every space, the last thing he'll see is not all the faces in the room but hers alone. The last thing he'll think about will be her hands; the last thing he'll feel is a pang of longing and fear twisted together, wanting so badly just to be safe in her arms. The last word he'll cry out, a cry of dereliction, will be, "Mama . . . Mama." His voice will grow softer as the fear grows sweeter. *Mama.* But no one will come. And he'll be gone.

* * *

"Go back to the pre-op room," said the counselor. "Just you and the boy."

I'm back in the original room. He's in the bed. No one else is there. The nurses are gone. The parents are gone. It's just me and him. Me—who is *him*—but from the future. He who knows precisely what he's about to experience. He who knows the pain that is to come—the pain when Joseph teases him, the pain when a girl screams "Ew!" and runs off laughing, the pain of asking out the same girl over and over and hearing the kindest of rejections every time. Here I am staring at the boy with his tussled brown hair about to be shaved, the skin on the side of his body about to be pierced, his bones about to be taken. He's in Bugs Bunny pajamas his mom made him; they have buttons so they can be worn when shirts can't be pulled over his swollen face.

"What do you want to say to him?" the counselor asked.

I continued to cry. I couldn't stop.

I watch the six-year-old boy look around and wait. As I try to think of what I should say to him, nothing comes to mind. Who better than me to tell this boy exactly what is about to happen in this moment or in his life? I am him. I know the path he's about to walk. I know the experiences he's about to have. I can tell him everything.

If I had something to say, it wouldn't be the right thing. It's not the Truth on the deepest level that can kiss and heal the Wound. He's so innocent. That's what I can't get over. None of this is his fault. He didn't choose to be born this way. Yet, because I'm him, I know how his innocence will be lost. He will hurt many people. And so much of that is because of this wound right here. There's nothing I can say that will avert it or change his mind. He won't understand what's about to happen. All the pain he's about to go through. The years of rejection. The ways he'll evolve and overcompensate. His addictions. His habits and focus. His need to achieve to earn love. His belief that people don't find him attractive. His self-loathing. His shame and rage. None of that will make sense to him because he hasn't lived it yet. I'm totally at a loss for how to communicate with him and comfort him as he sits there alone, slowly becoming more afraid.

So, unable to speak, I walk to his bedside and sit down next to him. Then I reach out my arms and pull him into my chest. I hold him tightly and weep into his hair—my hair. I cry for him and with him, and he hugs me back. But he doesn't understand my tears. He can't. He simply must live *through* it. Live *with* it.

It's too deep to explain to him. It's the Wound. Before it was his wound it was someone else's, but he's been pulled into its orbit. For him, the Wound is found in his face. And in this moment, all I want him to know is that I'm here. That I've come to him simply to be with him. I will never leave him, not for anything.

I came out of the vision, back into the room with Lindy. It was silent, marred only by the traffic and sirens on the New York streets. She was patient, simply letting whatever this exercise had stirred up in me marinate in my soul.

And then it hit me. As I envisioned the older me holding my younger self and crying into his hair, the truth surged up from deep in my gut. I knew what I wanted to tell him. It was a simple statement—myths always are—but as soon as it filled my consciousness, I knew it was the Truth that would kiss and heal the Wound. So back in the vision, I bent down, looked into his eyes that I knew so well, and said, "My boy, it's true. You're broken. You're so very broken. More broken than you even understand. You are not how you were supposed to be. And that will result in a lot of pain in your life."

My voice caught.

"But I need you to hear this next part because it's even more important. Yes, you are broken. But you are not ugly. Do you hear me? There's a difference. I choose you as you are. I will always choose you. I will never leave you."

"Where is Jesus?" Lindy asked.

I didn't answer her. Something lurched inside me again as it did at the start of this exercise, as it did in my recurring dream when a voice of resignation and apathy suggested life was a wasteland. In the vision, I sat on the bed alert, struck numb, holding the boy and jerking my head over to the corner of the hospital room where the adult me had stood just seconds before. For the briefest of moments, as briefly as I saw my mother before falling asleep, there was a flash of color, a silhouette of light, and then it was gone. The boy was gone. It was all gone.

I opened my eyes and looked at the tree in the backyard of this Hell's Kitchen apartment named "in the presence of God," and it made sense. I understood. It wasn't the adult me standing in the corner—it was Jesus. He was the one watching everyone do the best they could. He was watching me begin to experience what would become the central myth of my soul's wounded separation from God.

Jesus watches it all, unable to give a satisfying answer to anyone because it's all too deep. It's a truth from a spiritual realm that we simply can't understand yet. Someone else passed on the wound to us. We've been drawn into its orbit. And the wound called sin is now found in every person across the globe. My wound is found in my face and in the belief that I was ugly and unloved. The wound for you is in being abandoned by your parents, or rejected by your peers, or disregarded by society. The wound is the place where we were stripped away from the arms of God, no longer able to mirror our Father's loving face. It is in all of us, everywhere. It is our separation and our death.

But there was a way God could heal the wound. He had to enter the myth. So God took on flesh and entered my hospital room. He came to my bedside mourning, for it was all so broken. I wouldn't be able to understand, so he just wept into my hair, holding me tightly to his breast. His presence was all he could give me at that moment. But then God leaned down and looked into my eyes through the cross and told me, "It's true. You're broken, more broken than you realize. The brokenness goes deep. But hear me. You're not ugly. I will always choose you. I will be with you in the pain. I will be with you in your death. And we will do this together."

THE GOD WHO WENT FIRST

My friends, please go with me in this next part. Because it wasn't just that Jesus was at my bedside holding me and loving me as I was. That is wonderful, but it isn't complete. He could be lying. How do I know that God is telling me the truth that will heal my sinful separation from him?

Simply this: *the one who came to the bedside was also once in the bed.* As an adult, I could empathize with the pain the boy was about to experience. I was able to tell him everything about himself *because I was the boy.* I had already gone through all that he had faced. I'd had that surgery and came out the other side.

We can trust what God tells us about our wounded soul because he's already gone through it and come out the other side. The crucifixion story is the account of every human past, present, and future. It is the account of your deepest wound. No matter what it may be, you can be sure that God in Christ has already experienced it *exactly* as you have and defeated it.

As George MacDonald put it, "Jesus suffered unto death not that men might not suffer, but that their suffering might be like his, and lead them up to his perfection."[4] I believed myself to be ugly and worthy of rejection. Yet who is Christ on the cross but the disfigured one, rejected by his friends and enemies alike? Perhaps you were abandoned or abused. Who is Jesus but the abandoned one, the abused one? Perhaps you have always believed yourself deeply alone. Who is Jesus on the cross but the cosmically alone one? Perhaps horrible words were spoken to you as a child; Jesus was cursed and teased by leaders and passersby. Perhaps you needed someone to comfort you in a particular moment or season; Jesus needed his disciples to stay awake and pray with him, but they could not. Over and over, our reality and his reality are the same.

What is the myth from which all your soul's woundedness stems? It is whatever narrative you use to explain to yourself who you are and why you are as you are. And it's probably deeply painful. Where is it inside you? Look to it. Find its story. It will be a crucifixion. It will be the beginning of a deep wound and death in your soul. But look to your cross and see—*Jesus was there first*. That's the mysterious truth: you've never been alone, even if you felt like it.

Author Henri Nouwen wrote, "The question is not how am I to find God, but how am I to let myself be found by him."[5]

The answer is at his cross. There, and there only, you will be found as you are in the fullest measure of your being. For there, and there only, you will find God in the fullest measure of his being. He is the God with wounds. He is the God who went first. You will begin to experience this world differently because your old myth will be broken. To know that God is also broken but not ugly, that he is also abandoned but not forsaken, that he is also abused but restored does something inside your soul. It heals the deepest parts of you, and you begin to know yourself—who you are and why you are as you are—through a new myth. It is one filled with the presence and power of God's love inside the real, wounded you.

It was late 2017 when I finally met God as the God with wounds and heard him say he chose me as I was because he had already faced what I had faced. All the previous kisses had been but a balm for lesser wounds. On this day he offered the kiss for the Wound. I knew he spoke the truth. Because after he hugged me, crying into my hair, he looked at me and I saw his face was just like mine.

I came home and sat with Anna on the couch while our dog lay at our feet. I told her what happened in my session. As I recounted it all, I cried because I was so exhausted, embarrassed, and full of joy. Anna cried too. We held each other.

For this world was more brutal than we realized. And God was more daring and unsafe than we had imagined. It all was *Coram Deo*. Seeing how it happened, watching and marveling, I confessed, "Truly this has to be God's Son."

Eight

The God
Who Makes
Catastrophes
Good

It had been six months since that day with Lindy in *Coram Deo*. I struggled then and I struggle now to articulate the season that followed. The analogy I use is if you're on a ship that has been battered in a storm and finally crashes onto a beach. You find yourself lying on your back in the warm sand, the waves gently washing beneath you. The storm is over. The sun is out. You're going to live. But right now, there's no way you can move.

Something had happened in my body and soul that I couldn't understand yet, and it felt like I was just lying on the wet sand, eyes closed, absorbing the convalescing glow of the sun. It wasn't circumstantial. It was deep. In fact, the only circumstantial shift in my life that season was I stopped having the recurring dream. My sleep became deeper than usual. I still experienced moments of anxiety, fear, and the desire for control and validation, but something was *different*. For the first time, I *knew* I wasn't alone. I *knew* I wasn't ugly. The myth of my face and all its wounds, I now knew, was not true. I had said those words before, but they felt different on my tongue and in my heart when I said them now. My body knew it, not just my mind. God's grace had gotten to the root of me and had begun to move outward, redeeming the past where it had not been allowed before and affixing itself into the future where I was still to go. Slowly, invisibly, something had dislodged inside me. My world was shifting. One reality was cut off and withering away; another was born inside the old, filling the space bit by bit.

This new reality of broken-but-not-ugly life was being activated in different emotional spaces and the various wounds I have described, like new bloodborne oxygen rushing to the sight of the trauma to rebuild the tissue, repair my soul, and resurrect my life.

Two weeks after Easter 2018, I attended a conference in Midtown Manhattan. It was a conference for pastors, but it was a scaled back, unpretentious affair—a gathering of friends to pray together, worship together, and seek the Lord. I attended because our network, Hope Church NYC, was helping to put it on.

I had no expectation for God to do anything amazing in the room, much less in me. But on that first night, a British pastor spoke and shared her story. She and her husband had happily been Presbyterian pastors in England for a long time. However, one day she contracted meningitis. As she told it, a local group of "weird Christians" wanted to come pray for her healing and for God's power to work in her, which she emphatically did not want. Why? Because she knew that if they did they would speak in tongues, lay hands on her, and invade her space.

But they were persistent. Finding no way out of it, she dolefully gave in. They arrived on the agreed upon day and, according to her, proceeded to do everything she most feared. They laid hands on her, prayed in tongues, and invaded her space.

"It was awful," she recounted to the group that night. Allowing for a dramatic pause as she looked around the room, she continued, "The only problem was that I was cured of meningitis."

At those words, something popped inside me. Like a panic attack, but a good one. I began to breathe more heavily, and my hands started to sweat. But my vision seemed clearer. A bit alarmed, I looked around to see if anyone else was sensing this. I couldn't tell. But I was suddenly very aware that we were not alone in this room.

There was someone else on the beach.

A GOOD CATASTROPHE

J. R. R. Tolkien wrote an essay about the internal logic of fairy tales called "On Faerie Stories." His thesis is that we find these types of stories across culture and time, and they all possess the same themes, which are incidentally all present in the gospel story—the one true "faerie story" written into our hearts and revealed in Jesus Christ. Tolkien says that the highest purpose of faerie stories is to elicit joy. We think of joy as happiness that is plausible because circumstances can explain it. But that's not joy as faerie stories see it. Tolkien writes,

> The consolation of faerie-stories, the joy of the happy ending: or more correctly of the *good catastrophe*, the sudden joyous "turn"... is a sudden and miraculous grace: never to be counted on to recur ... it denies (in the face of much evidence, if you will) universal final defeat and in so far is gospel, giving a fleeting glimpse of Joy, Joy beyond the walls of the world, poignant as grief.[1]

Joy in fairy tales is a "good catastrophe." Tolkien calls this a eucatastrophe, *eu* meaning "good." It is a sudden and miraculous grace never to be counted on to recur. It is a moment in which all the evidence pointing toward death and defeat is reversed in an instant. It's a joy so unpredictable it feels as painful as grief.

We all have moments like these, but only a few. When a parent returns home from war and their kids crumple to the ground, weeping in emotion. When someone finally proposes unexpectedly and the person being proposed to can't remember a word of what was said. These are good catastrophes, a joy as painful as grief.

This is why the resurrection accounts of Mark are my favorite. Mark describes the resurrection for what it is—a *good catastrophe*. It is a joyous turn, a sudden and miraculous grace so contrary to the evidence that the first disciples experienced it as shock, grief, and trauma way before their minds could process any of it.

In Mark's account, the women arrive at the tomb heartbroken and confused. They find the stone has been removed. Their hearts start beating fast, their palms sweat, their breathing becomes shallow, and their pupils dilate. Something is very wrong. They rush into the tomb, and the panic within them drops into their stomach. Where Jesus' body should be sits a young man in a white robe.

We are told the women are *ekthambeō*, which means "to be struck with terror." The man says to them, paraphrased, "No need to be alarmed; you're looking for Jesus, the one who was crucified. He was buried here. But here's the thing—he's been raised from the dead. Go and tell his disciples and Peter that he's heading to Galilee, just as he told all of you before he died."

Mark says the women flee from the tomb trembling and *out of their minds*. The Greek word is *ekstasis*, which is where we get the word ecstasy from. *Ekstasis* is to be transported outside your normal paradigm of what is possible and impossible. You don't have language to understand what's happening. It's an entirely new calculus you haven't learned yet.

These women flee from the tomb in total shock. Their paradigm of life and death, possible or impossible, has been shattered. Mark adds this beautiful and seemingly unnecessary detail: "They said nothing to anyone, because they were afraid" (Mark 16:8). Unable to process what they've experienced, of course they're not going to say anything. They don't know what to say! Mark is describing what Tolkien has discovered: the resurrection is the great eucatastrophe.

For my mom's surprise sixtieth birthday party, Anna and I flew from Brooklyn to Richmond, Virginia. When she came around the corner and saw everyone, she froze. Then she put her head in her hands and wept for a while. She couldn't speak because she was in such shock that we were all in the room. In a sense, that moment was a resurrection. Good trauma gripped her as she encountered all those friends and family that she did not expect in her paradigm of what was possible for that day. It was a sudden and miraculous grace that sent her outside her body. Later, she told us it was so shocking she blacked out for some of the party.

But even my mom's party or parents returning from war or surprise engagements aren't quite like the resurrection of Jesus—just faint echoes of it, because each of them is still inside a larger paradigm of what's possible. Anna and I *could* jump on a plane; we *hope* soldiers come home; he sure as heck *better* put a ring on it. A resurrection is an even better eucatastrophe because it's *never* happened. But these examples get at an important point: our bodies experience resurrection before our minds understand them.

AN UNFORESEEN INVITATION

Back at the conference, the British pastor kept telling her story. Being cured of meningitis was a "good catastrophe" moment for her. Her paradigm of what was possible was shattered. Her paradigm of who God was and what he wanted out of this world was destroyed in an instant. If he is the God who raised a dead man back to life, it makes sense he could cure meningitis. But she never expected it. It was a sudden and miraculous grace, joy, and fear as painful as grief as she tried to process the implications of what this meant for her theology, her faith, her pastoral appointment, and her life.

As she spoke, she lovingly invited those of us in the audience to let God meet us in our doubts and fears, our failures and brokenness, and stretch us outward to call us beyond the safe confines of our paradigms. Basically, she said we serve a God of resurrection, a God who longs to foster good catastrophes in our lives. Whatever we imagine to be dead, God may have a second opinion if we will only allow him near us.

As she spoke, my "good panic attack" kept growing inside me. It had been two-and-half years since we settled in New York City, two years since we started building community at Hope Brooklyn, one year since our official launch, and six months since God met me in my wound at *Coram Deo*. And for the last six months, all the broken pieces of my wounded nature had sat in a tomb healing.

They were being stitched back together, though I didn't know it. There was a resurrection happening inside me that God was about to call forth. I hadn't come to this conference expecting anything. I felt like my energy was only now starting to return. But on this first night, as this kind and courageous woman spoke, something lurched inside me again. Like it was desperate to get out. I had no idea what was happening in my body. I only knew that I had one choice—yield to it or oppose it.

She finished her talk and encouraged us to enlarge our hearts on who God might be if he truly is the one who resurrected Jesus from the dead. It means he is closer to us than breath. It means he is with us in this space, alive, right now. His Holy Spirit is with us as we are, fully knowing us. It means his power is within us wanting to lead, use, and love us. And it means he wants to talk with us wherever we are, all the time.

"What is God saying to you?" she asked. My heart quickened. I felt very afraid. The answer came swiftly out of the pit of my stomach, like a presence that had been there the whole time but only now was given the ability to speak. *What is God saying to you?* The knowledge was released within me.

Ask, it said. My heart beat faster.

Ask for what? I replied internally.

For whatever you want.

THE RESURRECTION IS ABOUT A NEW REALITY

Jesus' resurrection is the claim at the heart of Christianity. But we don't jump to a resurrection. It's not within our paradigms. Upon one of Jesus' appearances to his disciples, Luke writes, "They were startled and frightened, thinking they saw a ghost" (Luke 24:37). A ghost! That's a possible conclusion. I mean, if you felt like you were seeing your loved one who had just passed you might say, "It's the ghost of my loved one." But Jesus quashed this interpretation. He answered them, "Why are you troubled, and why do doubts rise in your minds? . . . It is I myself! Touch me and see; a ghost does not have flesh and bones, as you see I have" (Luke 24:38-39). So, not a ghost.

It could also be said that the disciples were having a hallucination. This theory, taken up most notably by theologian Rudolf Bultmann, says that the disciples were in such a state of grief after Jesus' death and their betrayal that they experienced hallucinations of comfort and forgiveness to give them a reason to keep living. This isn't uncommon. People do sometimes claim to experience the loving presence of a recently deceased person they miss. But there are major problems with this viewpoint, best addressed by theologian N. T. Wright:

> If you had said to a first-century Jew that you had had a wonderful experience of the forgiveness (or the love and grace) of God, she or he would have been delighted for you. But if you had gone on to say that the kingdom had come, that a crucified leader was the Messiah or that the

resurrection had occurred, they would have been deeply puzzled if not downright offended. This language [of Jesus' resurrection] is simply not about private experiences, even communicable private experiences of forgiveness. It is about something happening within history that resulted in a world being now a very different place.[2]

The resurrection is about much more than just private forgiveness or grace. If the disciples were having a hallucination, that means they imagined a whole new system of God's kingdom being present in the world. An experience of grace and forgiveness is too soft an interpretation for a much more physical claim about a new earth, a new kingdom, the death of death and a new life happening in their own bodies and cities. It's hard to believe they could do all that simply for the sake of a "hallucination" that would lead them to be physically persecuted, socially ostracized, and martyred for their claims.

We tend to try to explain away God's miraculous power. I think it's because it's safer to accept our deaths than to believe another option is possible. We don't want to give into a foolish hope that disappoints us later and compounds the grief we're already experiencing. Like when we forgive and give the person a second chance—and they blow it again. Like when we decide to pray and trust God for that thing we've always desired—and it still doesn't come. Resurrection seems so impossible because death happens way more often. Even if it were true, it's safer for it to be true in theory rather than to expect it in our lives. The disciples were navigating this same thing. Maybe Jesus was a ghost. Maybe they were just hallucinating. Maybe it was only a psychological experience of relief to make sense of the heartbreak of the last few days. But that's not what the disciples claimed, and that's not what God says about his powerful presence in the world.

Jesus is not a ghost, nor a hallucination, nor an undigested bit of cheese. Jesus is, in some way, alive again, raised from the dead. It's not that it's impossible. It's just that it's statistically very unlikely—until it happens. It's a joyous turn, a sudden and miraculous grace, a joy as painful as grief. And my friends, I need you to hear this next part: death isn't the final word in your life, either. He's not a ghost. Not a hallucination. Not wishful thinking. He's the God of resurrection—a real life-over-death resurrection. A very good catastrophe.

A DRENCHING RENEWAL

Ask, it said. My heart beat faster.

Ask for what? I replied internally.

For whatever you want.

I breathed slowly as the band sang, shocked by the conversation I was having with God. I'd had encounters with God before, but not conversations. This was new for me. To have an experience where God jumps out of the book and is suddenly very real produced terror and shock in me. *Ask whatever you want*, the voice said. It was deep within me, not coming *from me* but *out of me*. It spoke to my soul, not to my mind.

Lord, I whispered, *I want you to put Anna and me on some-one's heart during this conference and have them reach out to us with a word from you.* A simple request. Honestly, I was embarrassed by it. It was too small. But after the pain of the last few years and the failure I had felt, it was all the faith I could muster in that moment. Even after God got to my central wound and told me he had always been there, who was I to ask for something grand? What if this was a hallucination to make sense of all the grief of the last few months? *Lord, I deserve nothing. If this is you, all I ask is you show me your love through someone else.* With that request, my hands touched the cold stone as I looked inside, saw the eyes of the man in white, felt his life and energy, and knew this was enough for now. The good panic attack went away.

The second day of the conference was full and worshipful. But nobody reached out to me with anything. Then the third morning came—our last session. As we entered the Salvation Army building with its high ceilings and brick walls, and as the band strummed their instruments and prepared to lead us in worship, I could already sense something different. There was a weightiness in the room. A stirring. My body was going somewhere my mind would not be able to follow at first, but it would understand later.

As the songs began, a stirring swept through me, or erupted out of me. I'd never felt something like this. My body was taken up into the movement of the room while my mind was watching it all happen, thinking, "What's going on? What is this sensation? Why can't I stop crying? Oh my gosh, I can't make it stop." I tensed up as a power swept through my body over and over like electrical currents going from head to toe and back again, reverberating within me. It was so strong that I couldn't move. I couldn't even breathe. I just convulsed.

Only the power convulsing me was *love.*

Tears fell, my emotions rendering me unable to sing. My first reactions, not thoughts, were feelings of unworthiness and relief. I felt like every spot of grunge and decay on my soul was being held up to a black light and shining out. But at the same time, I was met equally by a feeling of utter peace and release, like the relief you get when you're thirsty and drink a large cup of water. I had no idea how thirsty my soul had been. I had not realized how theoretical my faith had become, how devoid of intimacy—genuine, bodily intimacy with the living presence of God. How little my faith had been in the God of the Bible, the God who raised Jesus. Maybe I had never known intimacy like this because up until six months ago, I hadn't fully known God at the depths of his cross or mine. But as I stood tensed with God's love coursing through me, thoughts and emotions flowed together and took on the general shape of *gratitude.* I was thankful for this moment with God. I didn't want it to end, yet I wanted it to end in the worst way. I couldn't ask for anything more, yet I wanted the world too. I was so full of gratitude that his presence would draw toward me like this. I deserved none of it. And yet, *love, love, love, like waves gently washing beneath me, within me, over me.*

As I cried tears that couldn't come fast enough and thanked God with a tired and sober spirit, my heart shifted from kaleidoscopic intuitions, and suddenly I was back in the hospital room. Only this time, it was another hospital room. It was the room after "the big one." I saw myself as a sixteen-year-old boy reclined in another bed, strapped up to all the same contraptions as when I was six.

Like Ebenezer Scrooge with the Ghost of Christmas Past, I immediately knew the moment. It was the first time I had ever encountered God's Spirit. Up to that day I had been a follower of Jesus, but in that hospital room something new occurred. Just days prior I had undergone "the big one," and my face was very swollen and in a lot of pain. I had awoken from sleep and for whatever reason, seeing no one was in the room, panicked. Full of pain and sadness, I prayed something along the lines of, "God, where are you?" No sooner had I said that prayer than a current rushed over me—the same electric waves I was experiencing right then, thirteen years later. A current of love held me in gentle convulsions, gripped me like I was a child. I wept as the Spirit filled me to a breaking point, speaking to my body, "I'm here. You're not alone. I see you. I love you. You are mine."

SIGNS OF A CATASTROPHE THAT HE HAS MADE GOOD

I realize this may all seem so confusing. I don't know how many people have had experiences like the one I'm describing. I don't know how many have met God in the depths of their woundedness either, as I finally did. But I believe this part of the story is needed and helpful if only because it's true and it's what God did to me. God revealed a bit about his resurrection power and nature. But perhaps like you, I wasn't sure I could believe it.

A eucatastrophe—or a shockingly happy ending—sounds great and all, but it's called that for a reason. It's a sudden and miraculous grace that politely spits in the face of defeat. You'd be justified in being a bit skeptical toward my story if death seems most real in your own. Just like people were justified in being skeptical toward the disciples' claims. Just like the disciples were justified in their initial fear and skepticism.

When we surprised my mom on her birthday, why did she believe it was us? She knew us, for one. But then she came up and gave us a huge hug. She could tell we weren't a hologram but were really there in the room because she held us. When God acts in our lives in a eucatastrophic way, heals our wounds, and releases us to bear testimony to his power, how do we even tell the story in a way that people can recognize and believe?

The resurrection accounts show us. After the shock and terror of seeing an empty tomb and having weird experiences with a strange Jesus began to subside, the disciples still had to reach a place where they believed this was their rabbi raised to life. That something totally new was happening on the earth. How did they get to that place? Why were they so certain that the Jesus they were experiencing wasn't their collective grief or an experience of a mystical presence? What allowed their minds to catch up to their bodies? What was the thing that confirmed the good catastrophe?

"A week later his disciples were in the house again, and Thomas was with them. Though the doors were locked, Jesus came and stood among them and said, 'Peace be with you!' Then he said to Thomas, 'Put your finger here; see my hands. Reach out your hand and put it into my side. Stop doubting and believe'" (John 20:26-27).

The last stage of a wound's healing is called remodeling. After the initial trauma to the body, infection can set in. Once the infection is healed, the wound is covered by a scab to protect the healing within. During that process, the skin is suturing itself together from the inside out, the inflammation receding with no more chance of reinfection. Finally, when the time is right, the scab falls away—you could say a stone is removed—revealing new skin where there was once a gaping hole. However, this new skin looks different. It is clearly redder, fresher, even raised in places, and not the natural continuousness of the unwounded site. Though the area is healed and whole, there will always be the presence of a mark—a reminder that once upon a time, there was deep trauma in that spot. True, it cannot kill us anymore. It no longer has power to hurt us. But it was a real catastrophe and will always be there. The mark testifies to this.

In every Gospel account, Jesus does the same thing. He directs the disciples' stuttering, fearful, disbelieving bodies to look at and touch his own new one. And not just any part of his body but a very specific part—his hands, feet, and side. The disciples claimed he was resurrected because *Jesus' resurrected body had the scars from the crucifixion to prove it.* A scar points to a catastrophe. There was pain and death here. There was shed blood and grief and trauma. That's why Tolkien says the joy of a eucatastrophe is as poignant as grief. The two must share a common core, for the joy from the good catastrophe of resurrection can only emerge from the grief of the bad catastrophe of death.

The scars of Jesus are the signs that prove what was intended for evil has been defeated and suddenly and miraculously turned to our everlasting good. *Joy as painful as grief.* God is no longer the wounded God. He is now and always will be the scarred God too.

As I stood in a room full of pastors singing, I was unable to move, held captive by the current of love and the vision reminding me of that day in the hospital room. It was as if God was recapping our relationship up to this point. He was telling my body and soul how far he'd brought it. That I had never been alone.

The worship ended and the preacher came forward to deliver the final talk of the conference: the commissioning of those who were now sent back to wherever they served. He used the story of Gideon as his text. He spoke of how God took Gideon from the least tribe of Israel and the lowest family of that tribe and made him a warrior. Gideon's fame grew, and he was charged with leading a massive army of three hundred thousand men to battle. But God confronted him and said, "I cannot save you in battle, for you have too much." A stunning proposition. One would think that greater numbers would increase the likelihood of God achieving victory in Gideon's army. But this is the God who saves not through the world's mechanisms of strength but by identifying with the weakest, most broken parts of us and turning them to good.

God's strength is that he can bring life out of a catastrophe. *Gideon, you have too much for me to save you. You've forgotten that you came from the least tribe and the lowest family. You've forgotten that I save not by your strength but by mine, which is revealed in your weakness. You've forgotten that I bring life from death. Therefore, I'm going to take you back, before you had an army and before you had riches and before you believed in yourself, back to when you were nothing but a boy in a winepress from the lowest family of the smallest tribe, back when you had nothing but my word that said, "Go in the strength and power of the Lord."*

The preacher's voice began to swell and dance. That feeling of tenseness came over me again, electricity coursing through me with love and acceptance. "I'm going to take you back, pastor," he intoned to all of us pastors in the room, "back before you had a building, a launch team, or any funds, before you had the wounds from this difficult journey, before your church started to grow, back to when the church was nonexistent and you had nothing but the word of God that said, 'Go in the strength and power of the Lord.'"

As I wept, overcome with the truth of his words, God reminded me of all this. And it clicked. Scars are signs of a catastrophe that God has made good. Here was his Spirit coursing within me, resurrecting my life in ways I hadn't asked for because I didn't realize I needed it. It was a sudden grace, a joyous turn, and it was as painful as grief. But for me to believe this was God, he had to do it in a way that was attached to my deepest trauma, my bad catastrophe, my death. Which had always been held within my broken face.

The Spirit reminded me of that day when God first met me in the depths of my woundedness at sixteen, when I was at my lowest and felt uglier, lonelier, and smaller than ever before. It was a catastrophic pain. God was saying, "I brought life out of the depths of your pain then. I did it six months ago. I'll keep doing it. I turn your bad catastrophes into good ones. Know that this life is real—and boast in the scar of the catastrophes I make good."

The wound was finally becoming a scar. And as he brought so many threads together in my mind, the scab fell off and I could understand. I could see the scars of my soul shining forth from the scars of my broken-but-not-ugly face as the central sign to my place in God's story and in my testimony to Jesus being alive today. When I am asked to tell people how I know Jesus is alive, I point to my red lines, bumpy ridges, and misplaced bones and say, "Because he met me here. Because these marks are the signs of my greatest brokenness and my most glorious beauty."

When people ask you how you know Jesus is raised from the dead, don't point to your wealth, or your status, or your massive army. Point to the past addiction where Jesus met you. Point to the broken marriage where Jesus forgave you. Point to the insecure mess in your soul where Jesus said, "You are mine and I adore you. I went first so you can be free." Point to the scars. Point over and over and know that when we are weak, then miraculously, we are strong.

Gideon ended up leading an army of three hundred against thousands and winning. The point is simple: the world looked at Gideon's feeble army and laughed. But Gideon was holding up his scars to the world—scars of shame and weakness and death. And from them God brought life. The victory of God is not found in our strength but in our scars. Undeserved love from places of death gets the final word in our story. Your children. Your marriage. Your past shame. Your present suffering. Those places of inexplicable pain. He's there—if you'll let him meet you there. He will bring life out of death. Despite what you think you deserve, the final sentence of all things will be *love, love, love, offering a fleeting glimpse of Joy beyond the walls of the world, poignant as grief.*

Up until that last moment of the weekend, God had not answered my prayer from the first night. No one had reached out to me with a word from God. But as the preacher finished his sermon and all these threads came together in my mind and heart, my phone buzzed. It was a text from my friend David, the husband of the South African couple Anna and I met that very first snowy weekend in February three years ago. His text read, *Hey, friend. Felt God led me to this Scripture for you.*

> The wilderness and the dry land shall be glad;
>> the desert shall rejoice and blossom like the crocus;
> it shall blossom abundantly
>> and rejoice with joy and singing.
> The glory of Lebanon shall be given to it,
>> the majesty of Carmel and Sharon.
> They shall see the glory of the LORD,
>> the majesty of our God.
>
> Strengthen the weak hands,
>> and make firm the feeble knees.
> Say to those who have an anxious heart,
>> "Be strong; fear not!
> Behold, your God
>> will come with vengeance,
> with the recompense of God.
>> He will come and save you." (Isaiah 35:1-4 ESV)

A eucatastrophe.

Nine

The God Who Invites Us to Remove the Veil

Anna and I once went with Edwin Colon to a Narcotics Anonymous (NA) meeting in Brooklyn. We drove to one of those old historic buildings that gives Brooklyn the moniker "the borough of churches." Anna and I had never been to an NA meeting, so we were anxious about protocol, not wanting to embarrass Edwin.

We walked into a warmly lit room. A bare card table with coffee, mini sugar packets, and wooden straws sat at the door beside various literature aiding the recovery process. There were maybe thirty people present. As soon as we entered, about ten of them came over to greet us. Any anxiety we had was completely replaced by an acceptance in the room so thick we could grab it. We were met with handshakes and hugs and slaps on the back. One smaller woman beamed and extended her arms for a tremendous hug as soon as she saw us, as if we were family finally returning home. One elderly man asked if we wanted coffee and proceeded to prepare it for us. I was stunned at their warmth and kindness extended to complete strangers. In this room, there was none of the tension that existed outside these walls.

The program had a liturgical flow with announcements, a welcoming (but not calling out) of newcomers, a brief exhortation, and confession, which took up the bulk of the time. People stood up to say their name and how long they had been clean. "My name is so-and-so, and I'm celebrating two weeks/five months/twenty-two years today." People clapped no matter the length of time. Then they proceeded to share whatever was on their hearts—if they felt tempted or encouraged or sad.

The most heartbreaking moments were when people said they needed to give their time back because they had relapsed. This meant that even if they had been sober for ten years, they were setting the clock back to day one after their relapse. When they confessed this, a sound of grief filled the room and others whispered, "That's okay. Thank you for your courage. We're here for you." The person then shared what happened in an uncensored way, often crying as they explained how they weren't able to shut down their urges, self-deception, or pride before it was too late. When they finished and sat down, people grabbed their shoulders and told them, "Keep coming to these meetings. We're here for you." It was emotional.

After the time of sharing, there were some final announcements before the meeting finished. Anna and I got up to leave as Edwin mingled with people, letting them know there was a church built on the same principles that supplemented these meetings if they ever needed another community to support them in their journey.

No fewer than five people came over to hug Anna and me, though we hadn't said a word the entire evening, and told us to come back. They had no idea, I assume, that we weren't in the recovery process. They had no idea who we were because we hadn't said anything about ourselves. They simply extended friendship and love to strangers. It was emotional and overwhelming—in the best way possible.

THE RICHES OF THE CHURCH

Legend has it during the church's persecution under the Roman Emperor Valerian, a pastor named Lawrence was asked to hand over all the gold, silver, and valuable items the church owned. He requested three days to gather the "precious possessions of Christ." In that time, instead of gathering stones and metals, he gathered the broken and wounded of his church. According to accounts, there were men missing eyes and limbs and people with incurable diseases—the overlooked and marginalized in Roman society. When the Roman powers came to the church three days later to collect the gold, they were stunned to be met by such shocking company. At which point, Lawrence pointed to his brothers and sisters in Christ and said, "Behold the riches of the church—now take them."

Lawrence paid for this remarkable gesture with his life.

This is the genius of twelve-step programs, which were founded by Christians. The precise reason why people gather—the center point of their community and shared bond—is not their strength, riches, beauty, or success but their addictions, their wounds, and their brokenness that they confess they have no control over and are trusting a higher power to help them overcome. It does not matter if outside those walls they are a CEO, a celebrity, unemployed, or unknown. It does not matter if they are considered beautiful or ugly, intelligent or dumb. None of those markers of status matter. None of them are "true riches." Because inside those walls they are first one thing: a recovering addict whose life has become unmanageable and whose wound has been given over to the saving power of God. That is the glue of the community and the object of their boasting—the power of God dwelling in their soul's central wound.

"We are weak," they seem to say. "We have no control over our addiction, and we are meeting with others on this level ground. We are gathering around the shared wound, which we hope will become a scar as the healing process deepens in our lives. Through the power of confession, exhortation, candid vulnerability, and prayer, we are beginning to see the miracle happening: when we expose ourselves as weak, then he must be strong for us. When we let him into the center of all our suffering and death, we begin to taste his resurrection."

The truth is that we are forever tempted to pray, "Lord, heal us; Lord, make us whole!" But when we do, God points to the men missing eyes or limbs, those with incurable diseases, Martin and Luis and Patrick from Astoria, very old trees in quiet backyards, Amberly, Edwin, little Julie Zepeda flying through the air, and even little kids sitting alone and afraid in hospital rooms. And he says, "But can you not see it? I already have." The entire message of God found in Jesus is not that God has taken away our wounds and made us woundless—rather, God has joined us in the very center of our life's wounds and healed them, turning them into scars. Which means if the church does not gather around its scars, we don't gather with Jesus. *Our scars are the riches of his church—let us take them.*

THE LIVING SCARS ON THE BODY OF CHRIST

But where are they? We all have our unique marks based on the course of our lives, but where are the church's corporate scars precisely? I believe one interesting answer is that they're found in the sacraments. That's not so much a Protestant word, I realize. But whether Protestants know it or not, our worship services are filled with sacraments. Even our lives are filled with sacramental witness! Saint Augustine called sacraments "outward signs of God's inward grace." They are visible, material things that reveal an inner truth of God's presence.

We could say that the sacraments are scars that reveal an inner healing. They are the marks on Jesus' body that help us relearn how to live in this new world, no longer controlled by our wounds but free of their pain. As the church, we look at them every week, over and over, to remind ourselves we have already been made whole, are being made whole, and will be made whole. This is even more appropriate than we realize because at first glance, for those not in Christ and even for those who are, the sacraments do not appear beautiful or desirable but rather repellent and offensive. But the more we gaze at them, live them, and practice them, the more we see God's power shining out from them. There is sacramental power in confessing our sins and reconciling with those we have hurt or been hurt by. These are physical, embodied actions that reveal an inner gracious healing. There is also sacramental power in living lives of worship and prayer. Clark Pinnock points out, "We are impoverished when we have no place for festivals, drama, processions, banners, dance, color, movement, instruments, percussion, and incense. There are many notes on the Spirit's keyboard which we often neglect to sound, with the result being that God's presence can be hard to access."[1]

So much of life, when lived out of that deep place of God's presence in our wounds, becomes sacramental. But the church also engages in some important practices that bind our scars together with the scars of Jesus. And though there has been debate within the global church over how many practices there are, two primary ones stand out in the book of Acts and throughout early church history: baptism and the Lord's Supper.

Hope Brooklyn has been fortunate to baptize a number of people, but one day in particular was deeply impactful. The cafeteria where we ate brunch after service was decorated for the occasion. On the far end sat a long tin tub on top of a blue tarp, flanked by two fake olive trees. The tables of macaroni salad, charcuterie, veggies, hummus, and olives waited in the wings for the post-baptismal feast to cement these new and good interceptions in people's lives. The cafeteria was lined with long windows that welcomed in the bright March daylight.

There were Paul and Sierra, for whom the birth of their first son compelled them to surrender their lives to Jesus as witnesses that they could not love their son as he deserved but would receive God's love in their shortcomings and in their family.

There was Jared, who grew up Catholic. Hurt by his experience of Catholicism's rigid and hypocritical control over his life, he became an alcoholic to try to control something his religion could not. But in short order, he lost all control. Then he started coming to church and met Jesus, who placed himself into Jared's hands first, just like he had with John the Baptist and said, "Baptize me first." Jared's hands trembled and his voice wavered as he stood before the community and said he didn't want to be in control anymore. This love of Jesus was too powerful and gentle for his heart to stay cynical and angry any longer. And so he gave up control and went under the waters.

There was Aaron, a sixteen-year-old boy who knew God was for him but wasn't sure if he was worthy of God's love. Then he realized that this was precisely the point. He *wasn't* worthy. No one was. God didn't want the young man's worthiness but his heart, his life, and his love in return. God accepted Aaron, unworthiness and all.

There was Kathryn, who was baptized in another tradition at age five, the same year her dad died. She had lived a life of confusion and self-loathing. But something had shifted recently. When she thought of Jesus, all she could do was cry because she knew he wasn't disappointed or angry with her. As she gazed upon Jesus' scarred body, she knew in her bones that he really loved her, and she wanted to love him back just as she was. She sat in the tub and fell backward, giving herself up to the death-dealing waters.

There was Melina, who grew up in a portion of the church that claimed God wanted to save the world despite its sin, which meant we humans had to do the right things and avoid sin to earn God's salvation. But she had not done the right things no matter how hard she tried and how much she lied to herself and others. Like Kathryn, she met the Jesus who said, "I don't want you to do the right things. I just want you to let me love you, as you are, in the moments of your worst things. When you do, you'll find power and healing from those places. You'll find a love that no longer has time for the worst things."

Then finally there was Amberly, the first person I knew in Hope Brooklyn's story who gave her life to Jesus. As she stood before the community and spoke, tears streamed down her cheeks. "I didn't plan anything to say because I've been in denial that this is happening," she said. "I don't think it means that I'll stop having doubts or fears. I'm sure I will. I just think this means I'm promising to pursue Jesus for the rest of my life."

Yes. That is exactly what it means.

She stepped into the tub. As I held her hand, her body gave up its self-will. I prayed for her and the others. I asked her if she rejected Satan and his lies and schemes in her life. She said yes. I asked her if she surrendered to a loving relationship with God through Jesus in the center of her deepest wounds. She said yes.

"Then I baptize you, my sister, in the name of the Father and of the Son and of the Holy Spirit."

This is church.

The cafeteria was full, and there wasn't a dry eye in the space. Our worship leader strummed "Come Thou Fount" on his guitar, singing a tune or a chorus here and there. After every person emerged from the water dripping wet, the church erupted.

The community came over to hug each person tightly, not caring in the slightest that they were soaking wet. There was a joy that made no sense to those outside the church, I'm sure. These new followers of Jesus had just given up control of their lives. They had promised to not hide their wounds but to let God into them. To not hold anything back from him or the world but to boast of their weaknesses constantly. To let their scars be the most important part of their identities. That's not normal. It's not desirable at first. But it's liberating.

Behold the riches of the church—now take them.

At Hope Brooklyn we took the Lord's Supper every Sunday. When we hosted vision dinners with ten of us in a living room, we'd pass around half a loaf of bread, rip a piece off, and dip it in the cup that came behind it. When we transitioned to the Brooklyn Table at Next Steps Community Church, we'd end each discussion with Communion. When we began to meet in the school, the table holding the bread and wine sat front and center in the auditorium with the band and the preaching surrounding it, reminding all of us that this bread and cup were the only reason we gathered. Like the Narcotics Anonymous meeting with those gathering around their shared brokenness, we gathered around the sacrifice of Jesus' body and blood, reminding us that our only hope was found in what he did for us, not in what we could do for ourselves. At first glance it is a repellent sight: we are eating a man's flesh and drinking his blood. Yet here we encounter God's healing love shining out from the center of our most grotesque wounds, because they're now God's wounds too.

My friend Jon became a Christian during the practice of the Lord's Supper. After partying heavily one Saturday night, he arrived at church early the next morning, anxious to serve to atone for the previous night's wounds and, frankly, a season of them. Right or wrong, we try to do things for God, thinking he'll reward us with his love or at least not smite us if we say we're sorry. So Jon arrived at church and asked what he could do to help get ready for service.

"We've got things covered," I said. "But I could use help serving Communion at the end. Want to do that?"

He half gasped, half laughed.

"Absolutely not," he said.

But during the service, God spoke to Jon deep in his gut. It moved him. God said his love has absolutely nothing to do with our worthiness and everything to do with meeting him in our wounds—going deeper into our sin and finding he was there the whole time. God seemed to be saying, *Jon, if you can't meet me today in the state you're in, you'll never meet me at all. This is the ideal place for you to see me and understand how deeply I love you.*

After the message, Jon came up to me. Did he want to leave? Was he checking out?

"I changed my mind," he said. "I'll help serve."

Whatever balled-up resistance that had been stuck in Jon's gut dissolved. People came forward and received the bread while Jon and a few other servers said, "The body of Christ broken for you, the blood of Christ shed for you."

Only later in our friendship did I learn the true profundity of that moment. Jon had done cocaine the previous night. He told me that when you do cocaine, it lingers in the back of your throat for a while. Every time someone came up to receive the bread and cup and he said, "The body of Christ broken for you, the blood of Christ shed for you," he would taste cocaine in the back of his throat as his saliva trickled.

"The body of Christ broken for you." *Cocaine.*

"The blood of Christ shed for you." *Cocaine.*

"The body of Christ." *Cocaine.*

"The love of our wounded Savior Jesus Christ." *Cocaine.*

It was at that moment the light finally came on and he was overcome by the love of Jesus. Because after the night he had just chosen, after the season he'd been in, it was as if Jesus was saying, *You don't have to earn my love, Jon. You have already been perfectly loved by me, for I became just like you. I want you to know this love by serving my wounds to other wounded people all while tasting your own wounds trickling down the back of your throat.* When this reality welled up within him, it formed into a single question: How deep does the love of this God go?

To which I answer: behold the riches of the church—now take them.

UNVEILED FACES

In 2 Corinthians 3, Paul talks about this new relationship we have with God in Jesus. He likens it to Moses in the book of Exodus who, after coming down the mountain from being in God's presence with the law, had such glory on his face that he had to cover it with a veil so the Hebrews would not be terrified. Paul writes that if the law at Sinai, a covenant that brought death, could inspire such glory and awe, how much more could this new covenant in Jesus' love do so! He goes on:

> Therefore, since we have such a hope, we are very bold. We are not like Moses, who would put a veil over his face to prevent the Israelites from seeing the end of what was passing away. . . . But whenever anyone turns to the Lord, the veil is taken away. . . . And we all, who with unveiled faces contemplate the Lord's glory, are being transformed into his image with ever-increasing glory, which comes from the Lord, who is the Spirit. (2 Corinthians 3:12-13, 16, 18)

One of my favorite things as a pastor were the days I didn't have to preach at church. I simply participated as a member of the community. I was able to focus on Jesus without the pressure of having to preside. I was able, not as a pastor nor as a leader but as a son, to remove my veil, look into my true Mirror, and be transformed into the one I saw. I loved the end of the service when it was time for all of us to rise and take the Lord's Supper. The creaks from the old wooden chairs would sound like a chorus from heaven's B Choir as we slowly queued to the front. The music would play in the dim room. We'd walk forward, holding each other's shoulders, cheering each other on, mourning with those giving back their time, celebrating with those marking a new milestone in their relationship with God. We'd wait in line for our turn to confess that we were broken, weak, and wounded. God joined us, loved us, and healed us there, and we were no longer afraid. We took his body and blood proudly, for by the strength in his wounds we were made whole. In his scars, and in our own, we boast.

It was my turn to receive. Standing at the front, I looked into the brown eyes of a Jewish man. His left ear was crumpled, his left jaw disfigured. The left side of his face was maimed and scarred. But he smiled. He held out a loaf of bread and a cup of wine.

"Russell, will you receive my love?" he asked.

I nodded.

He leaned down and kissed the left side of my face. It was a long kiss. He wanted me to know and feel that he was kissing my wounded face. He was choosing to kiss it because he loved me. Not the me I thought I was or the me I should be, but the real me, the one I thought I had been hiding from him. The deformed, broken, weak, deceptive, humiliated, wounded me. He wanted to kiss that me. He wasn't repulsed by my wounds. He wasn't overlooking them. He saw them for what they were, and he knew there would be no me without them and the stories they told of my life. So he loved them. Because they made the real me. And he loved the real me.

He stood back up and looked toward the bread. I ripped off a piece and plunged my hand deep into the cup, the wine dripping onto the auditorium floor and splashing onto my shirt. When we all finished receiving, we began to sing loudly. Our laughter grew warmer and brighter.

And it won't stop. Because we still cannot believe that we never again have to be ashamed of how weak and broken we all are. Here in this space we hold up our scars. No one condemns us here. No one turns up their noses. There is always enough bad coffee and warm hugs to go around, and shoes piled high by the door.

Do you see him? Do you see his scars? Take off your veil. Let the world see your face. Let your scars shine. He is with you, even at your worst—*especially* at your worst. The strongest power in this world is God's love. It is not beautiful at first. People will not like it because it is a love that emerges out of death. It is a love found only in wounds, weakness, and surrender, for that is where God is now found in Christ. The world will not understand. When you remove that veil, they will be shocked. They may turn away out of fear. But you will know the truth. You can see what they cannot. There is fear not because your soul is grotesque but because you are aglow with the glory of Jesus shining out from your scars. So when the world cries out for healing, for justice, for salvation, for love, you need only look to Jesus' body, your body, his scars, your scars, and with an unveiled face answer, "Can you not see it? It's already done."

How do you know this?

"Look closer," you'll say. "His face is just like mine."

My Hope and Prayer

This journey of Jesus meeting me in my soul's wounds was perfectly timed. As society seemed to pressurize over these last few years, I found myself thrust even more into his presence. It has been another painful, refining season, though the pain is not due to infection but to strengthening. It's a good pain. The pain of rehabilitation. The pain of holiness, of becoming wholly God's. This deep relational knowledge of God's face to be like mine has changed everything.

During the apocalyptic year that was 2020, I sensed the Lord speaking a verse into my soul to give shape to what we were all witnessing. It came from the lips of Jesus and was directed toward the Pharisees. He said, "Isaiah was right when he prophesied about you: 'These people honor me with their lips, but their hearts are far from me'" (Matthew 15:7-8). I believe a revelation has come upon us all. That's what an apocalypse is in its original Greek sense—an unveiling of what's really beneath the surface. I believe our hearts have been revealed—what we truly love, who or what we trust with our lives, where we find meaning, where there are still open wounds in our souls, our true mirrors. And even though this unveiling is terrifying, it is also an opportunity to turn our wounded hearts toward Jesus. It's an opportunity for God to perform the same surgery on you that he performed on me. For in many ways, the stories in this book have simply been a revealing of the disconnect that had existed between my words and my heart. I said Jesus loved me. But my wounded and infected heart had little idea what that love truly meant.

All our pain can be traced back to unhealed wounds. I know how scary it is to discover there may be a gap between your words and your heart. Your mouth may boast one theology to hide a gaping wound in the center of your soul. But from that wound come all the questions that have explicitly or implicitly filled these pages. Does God really see and love *all* of me? Does he really choose me with my brokenness, sin, and wounds?

I hope by now you know the answer is a resounding *yes*. I hope you sense in your heart a joy trying to escape—the joy of knowing you're not alone and have never been alone. And you know this because now, I hope, you know that God's face is exactly like yours.

So I pray for you, reader. I pray there wouldn't be a single painful wound in your soul that can't be healed through Jesus' powerful love. I know now more than ever that he can do it. I know it like one who has intimately experienced it, tasted it, and walked it. I know that even though the pain seems final, it isn't, if only you would look a little closer. And if you peer a little deeper into your own soul, you'll find Jesus already there, having suffered your wounds to save, redeem, and heal you. He's already had the operation and made it to the other side. You're safe. You can be free. You can know what it's like to have no disconnect between your heart and your words, both of which boast scars.

When you do this, you'll learn a secret. When you know God's face is like yours, you start to heal from the inside out. You start to become wholly his, loving the Lord your God with all your scarred heart, soul, mind, and strength and your broken neighbor as your broken self. At a certain point, known only to the Holy Spirit, what becomes so striking is not just that God's face is like yours, but now *your face will start to look like his*. And the kingdom will become now, heaven will take shape here, and through a glass—though dimly—we with unveiled faces will reflect the glory of Jesus in new and miraculous ways.

Acknowledgments

I am grateful to many people whose words and friendship have helped shape the experiences and ideas of this book. To Anna—only you and only yours, my love. You have been the greatest gift of my life and, by God's grace, I look forward to many years journeying together kissing one another's scars.

To Nathan, your friendship haunts most every page in this book. Our partnership in planting Hope Brooklyn was such a wonderful surprise, and your kindness toward me as I experienced so much of this stuff in real time is one of the most indelible images of Christlike love I'll ever witness.

To Hope Brooklyn, and our many friends who were part of this story, thank you for being a people that embodied the conviction that wherever someone was in their spiritual journey, there was room at the table. Thank you for making room in your hearts for us and for the Lord.

Thank you, Drew Hyun, Pete Scazzero, Kristian Hernandez, Edwin Colon, and many other friends who loved me at my worst, let me love them at theirs, and showed me a different way. And thank you to the Emotionally Healthy Discipleship community, where so much of the language in this book was gathered.

Thank you to Bob Welch, whose encouragement led me to not give up on this project; to my literary agent, Greg Johnson, and WordServe Literary who took a chance on me; and to Al Hsu and InterVarsity Press, who believed in this story and helped sharpen it in ways I didn't know how.

There are so many more people to acknowledge. In lieu of naming them all, thank you for being to me as Paul and his companions were to the Thessalonians, who loved so much that they didn't simply share the gospel but their very lives (1 Thessalonians 2:8). Thank you for sharing your life with me.

Questions for Reflection and Discussion

INTRODUCTION: A LONGING FOR WHOLENESS

1. In what ways are you longing for wholeness in your life?

1. THE GOD WHO KISSES OUR WOUNDS

1. What are some wounds in your soul that have come from
   - something you were born with or born into?
   - something that happened to you?
   - something you did to yourself?
   - something you did to someone else or a group of people that also wounded you?

2. What would it look like to let God's love into those wounds just as Anna's love and kisses were directed onto my scarred face?

2. THE GOD REMINDING US WHO WE ARE

1. Have you ever experienced moments of transcendence that hinted at another reality than your own?

2. What would an interception of your wounded identity look like to know God is with you in every season and circumstance?

3. THE GOD WHO LIMPS IN AS A GUEST

1. Are there moments in your past when you used your power to get your way and ended up hurting someone else? Or what about when someone did that to you? How does that wound feel in your soul?

2. How might you live in a way that doesn't protect yourself with your own strength or power but lets God's strength protect you in your weakness?

3. What might it look like to live as a guest in God's world?

4. THE GOD AT THE BOTTOM OF THE WALL

1. What are some "markers of difference" you use to separate yourself from others? How is that separation metaphorically like sacrificing these other people or groups of people?

2. How is your soul affected knowing that Jesus has become the true sacrificial victim of us all?

3. What would it look like to build a new family of Jesus followers from the bottom of the wall, no longer

separating yourself from others but welcoming them into community to have Jesus remove the logs from their eyes?

5. THE GOD WHOSE RIB MAKES US WHOLE

1. Are you looking for a cure for your loneliness in either your spouse, a friend, or the idea of marriage?

2. What does it mean to you to let Jesus be your true *ezer kenegdo* as the foundation of all your relationships in the world?

6. THE GOD WHO PERFECTLY LOVES OUR IMPERFECTIONS

1. In what ways do you try to control your image and how people think of you?

2. What would it look like to be seen in all your imperfections and know Jesus has loved you perfectly in those places?

3. What might celebration look like in your life as a way to push back against what people expect of you? How might you join Jesus in his joy?

7. THE GOD WHO WENT FIRST

1. Is there a central myth in your life that you find yourself constantly returning to as an answer for why you're unlovable, broken, or wounded?

2. What would it mean to imagine that moment or season as a crucifixion and find that Jesus experienced it first and beat it so you can trust you will beat it in him too?

8. THE GOD WHO MAKES CATASTROPHES GOOD

1. Have you ever experienced a eucatastrophe? What did it feel like in your body?

2. What would it look like for God to bring resurrection power into your soul and life in real, tangible ways each day?

9. THE GOD WHO INVITES US TO REMOVE THE VEIL

1. In what ways does your church or spiritual community gather around corporate scars?

2. In what ways does your church or spiritual community gather around its strengths instead of its weaknesses?

3. What does it mean for you to remove the veil on your life and let the glory of Jesus shine out from your scarred soul?

Notes

1. THE GOD WHO KISSES OUR WOUNDS

[1]Alice Miller, *The Drama of the Gifted Child* (New York: Basic Books, 2008), 27.

[2]Miller, *Gifted Child*, 28, emphasis mine.

[3]Henry George Liddell et al., *A Greek-English Lexicon* (Oxford: Clarendon Press, 1996), 77.

[4]Robert Wilken, *The Spirit of Early Christian Thought* (New Haven, CT: Yale University, 2005), 21.

[5]St. Athanasius, *On the Incarnation*, trans. Archibald Robertson, 2nd ed. (London: D. Nutt, 270–271 Strand, 1981), 93.

2. THE GOD REMINDING US WHO WE ARE

[1]Michael Specter, "Partial Recall," *The New Yorker*, May 2014, www.newyorker.com/magazine/2014/05/19/partial-recall.

[2]Jonah Lehrer, *Proust Was a Neuroscientist* (New York: First Mariner Books, 2008), 85.

[3]Rabbi Jonathan Sacks, *Covenant & Conversation: Exodus* (New Milford, CT: Maggid Books, 2010), 1.

[4]Anne Lamott, *Bird by Bird* (New York: Anchor Books, 1994), 200.

[5]C. S. Lewis, *The Weight of Glory* (New York: Harper Collins, 1949), 42.

[6]Ranier Marike Rilke, *Rilke's Book of Hours: Love Poems to God* (New York: Riverhead Books, 1996).

[7]James K. A. Smith, *How Not to be Secular: Reading Charles Taylor* (Grand Rapids, MI: Eerdmans, 2014).

[8]Rachel Herz, "Remembering the Scent of a Meal," *Talk of the Nation*, NPR, November 26, 2010, www.npr.org/2010/11/26/131608865/remembering-the-scent-of-a-meal.

[9]*The Didache*, IX.

3. THE GOD WHO LIMPS IN AS A GUEST

[1]Willie Jennings, *The Christian Imagination* (New Haven: Yale University Press, 2010), 43.

[2]Francis Brown, Samuel Rolles Driver, and Charles Augustus Briggs, *Enhanced Brown-Driver-Briggs Hebrew and English Lexicon* (Oxford: Clarendon Press, 1977), 7.

[3]Brown, Driver, and Briggs, *Hebrew Lexicon*, 438.

[4]Brown, Driver, and Briggs, *Hebrew Lexicon*, 429.

[5]Emily Belz, "The Love is Here," *World Magazine*, January 17, 2019, https://wng .org/articles/the-love-is-here-1617299583.

[6]C. S. Lewis, *The Great Divorce* (New York: HarperOne, 1946).

4. THE GOD AT THE BOTTOM OF THE WALL

[1]Andrew T. Lincoln, *Word Biblical Commentary: Ephesians* (Grand Rapids, MI: Zondervan, 1990), 1-4.

[2]Krista Tippett, "Jean Vanier: The Wisdom of Tenderness," *On Being with Krista Tippett*, December 20, 2007, https://onbeing.org/programs/jean-vanier -the-wisdom-of-tenderness/.

[3]T. S. Eliot, *The Rock* (New York: Harcourt, Brace, and Company, 1934).

[4]Larry Hurtado, *Destroyer of the Gods* (Waco, TX: Baylor University Press, 2017), 90.

[5]Tom Boylston, *The Stranger at the Feast* (Oakland: University of California Press, 2018).

5. THE GOD WHOSE RIB MAKES US WHOLE

[1]Elizabeth Kolbert, "Why Facts Don't Change Our Minds," *The New Yorker*, February 19, 2017, www.newyorker.com/magazine/2017/02/27/why-facts-dont -change-our-minds.

[2]Robby Berman, "Your Brain Interprets Prolonged Loneliness as Physical Pain—Why?," Big Think, January 6, 2017, https://bigthink.com/health/the -powerful-medical-impact-of-loneliness/.

[3]Michele Kroll, "Prolonged Social Isolation and Loneliness are Equivalent to Smoking 15 Cigarettes a Day," University of New Hampshire, May 2, 2022, https://extension.unh.edu/blog/2022/05/prolonged-social-isolation -loneliness-are-equivalent-smoking-15-cigarettes-day.

[4]Sherry Turkle, *Alone Together: Why We Ask More from Technology and Less from Each Other* (Philadelphia: Basic Books, 2017).

[5]David Bentley Hart, *The Experience of God: Being, Consciousness, and Bliss* (New Haven: Yale University Press, 2013), 107-10.

[6]Francis Brown, Samuel Rolles Driver, and Charles Augustus Briggs, *Enhanced Brown-Driver-Briggs Hebrew and English Lexicon* (Oxford: Clarendon Press, 1977), 740.

[7]Christopher West, *Theology of the Body* (West Chester, PA: Ascension Press, 2004).

[8]C. S. Lewis, *Mere Christianity* (New York: HarperCollins, 1952), 148-50.

6. THE GOD WHO PERFECTLY LOVES OUR IMPERFECTIONS

[1]"Alcohol and Drug Misuse and Suicide and the Millennial Generation—A Devastating Impact," *Trust for America's Health*, June 13, 2019, www.tfah.org /report-details/adsandmillennials/.

[2]Will Storr, *Selfie: How the West Became So Self-Obsessed* (London: Picador, 2017), 7.

[3]Storr, *Selfie*, 8.

[4]Storr, *Selfie*, 10.

[5]Mark O'Connell, "The Deliberate Awfulness of Social Media," *New Yorker*, September 19, 2018, www.newyorker.com/books/under-review/the-deliberate -awfulness-of-social-media.

[6]J. R. R. Tolkien, *Letters of J. R. R. Tolkien* (New York: Houghton Mifflin Harcourt, 2000).

[7]Barbara Ehrenreich, *Dancing in the Streets: A History of Collective Joy* (New York: Henry Holt and Company, 2006), 65.

7. THE GOD WHO WENT FIRST

[1]"Joseph Campbell and the Power of Myth—'Masks of Eternity,'" Bill Moyers, June 26, 1988, https://billmoyers.com/content/ep-6-joseph-campbell-and-the -power-of-myth-masks-of-eternity-audio/.

[2]Joseph Baumgartner, "Myth and Mythology," *Philippine Quarterly of Culture and Society* 2, no. 4 (December 1974): 195-200.

[3]Leonard Mlodinow, *Subliminal* (New York: Random House, 2012), 8.

[4]George MacDonald, *Unspoken Sermons: First Series* (Shippensburg, PA: Sea Harp Press, 2022), 16.

[5]Henri Nouwen, *The Return of the Prodigal Son* (New York: Doubleday, 1994), 106.

8. THE GOD WHO MAKES CATASTROPHES GOOD

[1]J. R. R. Tolkien, "On Faerie Stories," *Essays Presented to Charles Williams* (Oxford: Oxford University Press, 1947), 14.

[2]N. T. Wright, "Christian Origins and the Resurrection of Jesus: The Resurrection of Jesus as a Historical Problem," *NT Wright Page*, 1998, https://ntwrightpage .com/2016/07/12/christian-origins-and-the-resurrection-of-jesus-the-resurrection -of-jesus-as-a-historical-problem/.

9. THE GOD WHO INVITES US TO REMOVE THE VEIL

[1]Clark Pinnock, *Flame of Love: A Theology of the Holy Spirit* (Downers Grove, IL: InterVarsity Press, 1996), 37.

About the Author

R ussell Joyce is the national director of church planting for the Foursquare denomination and senior pastor of Faith Center in Eugene, Oregon. He has held both roles since mid-2021.

He is cohost of the *Same Jesus* podcast with his friend Dr. A. J. Swoboda, providing resources and tools on relevant topics for pastors both within and outside the Foursquare movement.

He currently lives with his wife, Anna, and two sons, George and Simon, in Eugene, Oregon.

Website—https://www.russellwjoyce.com

Instagram—@russellwilliamjoyce

YouTube—@faithcentereug

Podcast—*Same Jesus* by The Foursquare Church

For all inquiries—rjoyce@foursquare.org